A COURSE IN MIRACLES IN 5 MINUTES

Personally using the principles
of A Course in Miracles
to change your life.

© Jerry Scars 1994

Associates Publishers
San Diego, California

ISBN 0-9639741-0-6

Library of Congress Cataloging-in-Publication Data
Sears, Jerry
A Course in Miracles in 5 Minutes
San Diego: Associates Publishers, 1994
Summary: An explanatory workbook used by those seeking
the benefits of the metaphysical New Age "A Course in Miracles".
    160 p.   19 cm.
Workbook
    Includes index. Based on A Course in Miracles publication by the Foundation for Inner Peace.
    1. Attitude (Psychology) 2. Mental Healing 3. Spiritual Life
    I. Title II. Foundation for Inner Peace
BX9998.S** 1994   93-091021
230.99 – dc   CIP

Portions from *A Course in Miracles* © 1975, reprinted by permission of the Foundation for Inner Peace, Inc., P.O. Box 1104, Glen Ellen, California 95442. *A Course in Miracles* may be purchased from your bookseller or from the Foundation for Inner Peace. The three volume hard cover set is $40. The single volume (all in one) soft cover is $25. The hard cover (all in one) is $30.

Manufactured in the United States of America

Cover Design by Lisa DeCarolis
Typography by Imagine

First Edition, February 1994
10 9 8 7 6   5 4 3 2

This book may be ordered from your bookseller, or from Associates Publishers, using the order blank at the back of this text. Or, write to: Associates Publishers at 16776 Bernardo Center Drive, Suite 110B, Rancho Bernardo, CA 92128. The cost is $12.95 plus $3.00 domestic or $5.00 international shipping for 1 book. Add $0.50 domestic or $1.00 international shipping for each additional book in the same order. Volume discounts are available.

Also by Jerry Sears:

    Career Miracles

I dedicate this book to my daughter Liz,
who always remained loving...
even when her dad was not.

Table of Contents

Directory of Exhibits iii

Acknowledgments v

Forward vii

Chapter 1
How A Course in Miracles Replaces Pain With Joy 1
    Completing the exhibits in this book 2
    Measuring your basic beliefs 4

Chapter 2
Why Does it Hurt? 15
    Your life mirrors your beliefs 15
    The Course has only one answer 18
    The Course versus motivation systems 21
    Low self esteem - the curse of this planet 22

Chapter 3
When it Hurts 31
    The inner conflict 31
    Our beliefs cause our conflicts 34
    The road to peace 37
    "Achievement versus spirituality" 39

Chapter 4
Can I Actually Improve My Self Image? 47
    Why the Course works 47
    Anger as your indicator 48
    We make our own world 52

Chapter 5
Applying Course Principles to Your Relationships With People 55
    How the Course differs from other belief systems 59

The absence of "Sin" 62
Measuring your belief in "Sin" 62
Measuring your "little willingness" 65
Evaluating your answers to the seven "sin" questions 65
Why your mind changes your world 67
Measuring progress using Course principles to change your mind ... 68
Escaping a world of bigotry 72
Using the belief - life changing questions 72

Chapter 6
How the Course Eliminates Fear and Helps You to be Open 75
Knowing your fears 75
Comparing your fears to those of others 77
Understanding your basic beliefs 80
Measuring change 85
Another way to compare your results 88

Chapter 7
Practical Applications at Work 91
Is the love principle applicable everywhere? 92
Belief changes versus interpersonal skills 93
Fear blocks using "people skills" 98
The difference in Course versus skill beliefs 98
Applying Course beliefs at home 100
My own experience 102
Looking at your own family in Course terms 103

Chapter 8
The Miracle of Healing the Blind Beggar 111
The Course in a nutshell (or at least in four exhibits) 111
Is the journey worth the trouble (or should I not make the trip)? ... 114
The Course solution to the belief-fear-pain cycle 117
Your problems are your gifts 119
Your final task on the road to being a HLCG 126

Index 133

Directory of Exhibits

Some exhibits have the same title. This is because they are presented first for you to complete, and then again with sample answers. Those exhibits with three of the same titles result from giving you two different sets of sample answers. In all the exhibits, you are urged to complete the "fill-in" exhibit first and then, after doing this, to look at the sample answers.

Chapter 1
1a   Measuring Your Basic Beliefs 5

Chapter 2
2a   My Feelings as a Guide in Applying Course in Miracles Beliefs 17
2b   My Feelings as a Guide in Applying Course in Miracles Beliefs 20
2c   Steps to Higher Self Esteem 23
2d   Your View of the World (another way of looking at anger vs. joy) 25
2e   How My Perception Flows from My Self Image 27
2f   How My Perception Flows from My Self Image 29

Chapter 3
3a   How I Seek Myself in Others 33
3b   How I Seek Myself in Others - a non-course view 36
3c   How I Seek Myself a Course in Miracles View 38
3d   My Beliefs as an Achievement Striver 40
3e   My Worldly Beliefs as an Achievement Striver 42
3f   My Course Beliefs as an Achievement Striver 45
3g   Comparison of this World Belief Results to Divinity Results 46

Chapter 4
4a   Four Major Events Causing My Anger and the Reasons Why 49
4b   Four Major Events Causing My Anger and the Reasons Why 51
4c   Four Major Events Causing My Anger and the Course Answers 53

Chapter 5
5a   How My Relationships Evolve 56
5b   How Relationships Evolve - Worldly Answers 58

5c   How Relationships Evolve - Course View 61
5d   Checklist of Beliefs in Relationship Joy vs. "Sins" 64
5e   Changes in Your Life from Changes in Your Beliefs 69
5f   Changes in Your Life from Changes in Your Beliefs 71

Chapter 6
6a   Fears vs. Benefits from Being Open 76
6b   Fears vs. Benefits from Being Open 78
6c   Fears vs. Benefits from Being Open - Course View 79
6d   What Should I be Open About? 81
6e   My Ranking of My Beliefs about Famous Sayings 82-83
6f   What Should I be Open About? 87
6g   What Should I be Open About? 89

Chapter 7
7a   Personality Characteristics in a Typical "People Skill" Training 95
7.1b Personality Characteristics in a Typical "People Skill" Training 96
7.2b Personality Characteristics in a Typical "People Skill" Training 96
7c   Personality Characteristics in a Typical "People Skill" Training 99
7d   Three Things I Like Worst and Best about My Family 104
7e   Three Things I Like Worst and Best about My Family 106
7f   Three Things I Like Worst and Best About My Family
         A Course in Miracles Perspective 108

Chapter 8
8a   Obstacles to be Overcome 112
8b   Three Steps in Measuring My Progress 112
8c   My New View of My World 113
8d   In Using the Course Road Map, I Believe 113
8e   My Belief, Fear, Pain Scale 116
8f   My Belief, Fear, Pain Scale 118
8g   A List of My Five Most Difficult Problems 121
8h   A List of My Gifts Arising out of My Fears 123
8i   A List of My Problems 124
8j   A List of My Gifts Arising out of My Fears 125
8k   Worksheet for Applying Course Principles to Problems 126
8l   Worksheet for Applying Course Principles to Problems 127
8m   Worksheet for Applying Course Principals to Problems 129

Acknowledgments

This book exists because of the contributions of many kind people, including hundreds of people in the Course, around the world. I would like to thank them all, while taking the responsibility for content and errors myself. Among them are: Bob Draper, Paul "Buddie" Gilstrap, Richard Roskin, Bill Atkins, Lou Crucione, Carl Parks and the hundreds of my Course in Miracles students who have been my finest teachers but most particularly to Hossana von Salem for her dedication.

I have tried to reflect this age of female emancipation by eliminating the use of the masculine tense. However, there are certain limitations in the current use of English which make this difficult. Therefore, I apologize for any verbal sexism. It is not intended. My beliefs are those of the Course. The only real gender differences are physical, such as plumbing.

Foreword

This is a guidebook to A Course in Miracles. It has been written for those who want to enjoy the peace the Course has to offer. This guidebook is a method of starting in the Course by determining your specific needs. It is for those who may have found the language of the Course itself either difficult or intimidating. I have taught a class in the Course for a number of years, and have attended hundreds of others. In doing this, I have seen a wide variety of responses to the Course.

The most common comments from those who find the Course difficult are that: 1) the language of the Course can be difficult to grasp, and 2) the Course can be academic, as opposed to practical, in its presentation. Many people go forward anyway because the Course offers them a way out of their pain. I hope that this guidebook can be used to bridge these two problems. It is NOT intended however, in any sense, to replace the Course itself, since nothing can do that. The liberal use of self testing exhibits throughout is intended to help in using this book in five minute intervals. The subject of all exhibits is you. If you get stuck on an exhibit, stop and take a break.

The thrust of A Course in Miracles in 5 Minutes is to apply the Course to you. If you do not personally apply it, you will not benefit from it. Studying the Course academically is like taking a course in art appreciation or computer science without ever using a paint brush or computer. Your own belief system is the canvas on which you will create. Your mind is the computer which needs programming and data input. At the other extreme from academic study is a totally participatory sensory, and sensuous, approach. This "touchy, feely" sing-dance-clap approach feels great, but gives little other benefit. It is like giving the artist (you) a brush or a computer without the benefit of instruction. Many times, this approach is a substitute for addressing the issues causing the problems. In this sense, it can be like Valium or Prozac, masking the symptoms instead of solving the problem. There is a middle ground for which we are striving.

This guidebook is intended to be used together with the Course. It is solely a way of gaining perspective on where you are compared with the views of the Course. As such, it covers the two main issues addressed by the Course: ego belief (pain of low self esteem) versus God belief (assurance of joy). My intent is to lead you through the beginning of the Course. This can be the most difficult part. Best estimates are that about four million people have started the Course, to date. They did so without this book, so it is far from a necessity. I hope that this book might: 1) reduce the time, and/or 2) increase the number of people, who reach the joy offered by the Course.

Perhaps, my personal experience may help. I came into the Course after the failure of my second marriage and some significant business reversals. I was in my fifties and didn't know who I was. The pain of my financial and marital problems was intense. That pain reflected a lifetime of such issues. I had been through many forms of therapy, none of which had really worked.

My self esteem was so low that I could not imagine how to boost it. As a result, my world was difficult, painful, negative and unproductive. Since, as the Course says, the world we experience is but a mirror of our own belief system, my world could be nothing else.

Most people (including me) seek the Course because their lives are not working and/ or their pain is too intense. I had created my own repetitive victimizations. By doing so, I ensured that my childhood pattern of persecution was repeated. I had grown up in a very poor family. My mother was born in Italy and had immigrated to this country as a child. She met my father while she was attending classes at Boston University and he was in law school there.

Since he came from a very religious Jewish family, and she from an equally religious Catholic one, there was intense conflict, resulting in an almost simultaneous divorce. Of course, both families rejected each other with an intensity reserved only to the Godly and righteous. I never met him. When I tried to meet his family years later, I was rebuffed as "a Catholic and therefore a Christian."

These events are all demonstrative of the Course's theme of the insanity of this world. They can only flow from a world which sees a God capable of anger, rather than only of love. This is why the unique Course belief in a God only of love is so fundamental to understanding how to apply the Course. You cannot experience both joy and anger at the same time.

My mother was poor, alone and needed work. I was sent intermittently, at a very young age, (grades 3 through high school) to a series of Catholic and "religious" right wing Protestant boarding schools. At these schools I learned, painfully, the prejudice directed at minorities and Jews, particularly defenseless ones (this being permissible only by my and their belief in an angry God).

The violence, beatings, death threats, and sexual molestation were all directed at me as the nearest thing to a defenseless Jew reasonably available. Unlike most real Jews, I had no family to turn to. My mother simply could not believe that "men of God" could do such things. Of course, we in the Course know that men or women who believe in an angry God are capable of doing anything in the name of that God. It does not make any difference whether they are Christian, Jewish or Muslim. My "punishment" resulted from blame by the "righteous." The Course tells us this: "Any concept of punishment involves the projection of blame, and reinforces the idea that blame is justified." (Text P. 88).

I can clearly remember the "preachers" at these various schools, both priests and ministers, preaching from the pulpit that since the Jews killed Christ they deserved to suffer, die, etc. These were particularly bad Sundays for me because it was then that, as a child of 8 to 12 years, I would be the subject of the highest levels of violence. On these days I would also get the most death threats. The promise was most often that I would be killed in my sleep.

I obviously was not killed, but I did suffer severe repeated physical beatings, deep sexual molestation and penetration by both teachers and older boys. This was all done by "religious" people who were in schools devoted to the word of God. Their "God" however, was an angry God. Belief in an angry God will support any behavior, no matter how extreme or aberrant.

That this could happen to a child in the name of God is, of course, not surprising to any student of the Course. The Course teaches us the basic principle that this an insane world. It also teaches us that when one believes that there is a God capable of anger, one can justify any behavior in the name of that God. "In this world one is supposed to 'forgive' these perpetrators." In the world of the Course there is nothing to forgive. The Course calls such anger "projection." It is projecting ones own insecurities onto others. This high a level of anger is explained as follows: "...that is why those who project are vigilant for their own safety. They are afraid that their projections will return and hurt them." (A Course in Miracles - Text P. 121).

The level of my "forgiveness" is measured by my continuing pain. The lifetime time bombs that can be left with me were the: fear of being murdered if revealed as having a

Jewish father, fear of men and total lack of self esteem. None of these is a particularly positive aid to functioning in society.

I tried many therapies and their therapists over many years, but nothing really worked until the Course. The Course has solved most of these "gifts" from believers in an angry God. Perhaps this is because of a basic position of the Course: that we are not a body. The Course explains why a spiritual approach to pain can work when a traditional therapeutic one will not. It is the basic belief: "Glory is God's gift to you, because that is what He is. See this glory everywhere to remember what you are." (A Course in Miracles - Text P. 133).

Most traditional believers in a God who has the capacity to be angry, have an internal built-in conflict. They want to be, and believe themselves to be, loving, kindly disciples of a belief system (monotheistic) that stands for high moral values. They exude love for their fellow man. However, the definition of their fellow man is often restricted to people who share their spiritual views.

This restricted view of their fellow man flows directly from their belief in the possibility of an angry God. The ego, or in their terms, the devil, causes them to view their specific belief as a quasi-exclusive path to God. This enables God's anger to condemn those who don't walk their path. The Course answers simply that there are a thousand paths. None of these are any "better" than others. Some are simply faster.

Fundamentalists of any persuasion seem to believe that the Course is too "new age." The "new agers" seem to feel that it is too Jesus oriented. How fortunate we, in the Course, are to be in the middle. As you go through this material, remember this middle road of the Course and its basic principles: 1. let love replace anger, 2. God is love (not anger), 3. forgive your brother for what he did not do to you, 4. there is no sin, only mistakes, 5. this is a world of insanity, created by us, not God, 6. your perception creates your reality, and 7. there are a thousand paths to God.

My own journey through the Course can illustrate this, and so I will share some parts of the Course in my own life. The first part of my life is an example of how not to apply any one of these Course beliefs. I grew up with my childhood implanted decision that should anyone discover that my father was Jewish, I would be killed. Thus as soon as possible I changed my name and tried to be as WASPish as possible. In doing this, I lost the gift that God had given me and dismissed it, vividly showing me the insanity of this world. I went for the power (insanity) of this world as my protector.

The Course tells us clearly that the world we experience is the one we create. I carried lots of fear, hatred and anger. That, therefore, is what I experienced. The only people in my life were those who had elected to live their lives in anger, since I would tend to screen out anyone else. The Course says, "From your perception flows your reality," or more directly:

"What I see in my brother is what I want to see in him, because it stands for what I want to be the truth. It is to this alone that I respond ... and only this."
(From: A Course in Miracles - Lesson 335)

As you go through the table of contents to this book, you will see the Course as it unfolded for me. In my experience, most people get into the Course because of the pain in their lives.

Because I wrote this to help people into the Course, it is replete with exhibits. These are "fill-ins" and intended to be used. The words of this book are far less important than your use of these exhibits. Respond to the questions or statements. It is this that gives this book any value it may have.

The title "A Course in Miracles in 5 Minutes" results from the use of these exhibits. My hope is that by having them with you (some can be copied), and taking five minutes here and there, you will grow in these principals. These exhibits are designed as well to bridge the gap between the academic presentation of the Course and applying the Course to your own life. The five minutes does not mean that five minutes from now you will achieve the peace we all seek.

San Diego, CA, February 14, 1994

Chapter 1

How A Course in Miracles
Replaces Pain With Joy

A Course in Miracles appears to be about "God." In the sense of traditional religion, it is not. It is about a God who is not capable of anger. It is much more about pain versus joy. The absence of anger is what enables the Course to be a path from pain to joy. The Course itself says that there are a thousand paths. This one may, or may not, be for you. This is a course in mind training. The training leads us along through these truths:

1. There are lots of things we don't know or understand; we may know as little as 1% of the "knowledge of the universe".
2. If your life is working (ie: you are not in too much pain) you don't tend to seek further knowledge, ie: a belief system that works for you–unless you are just in the knowledge business.
3. If you are in enough pain, you will keep searching until you find an answer to abate your pain and bring you some measure of joy.
4. That answer may come to you in a materialistic, fundamentalist or metaphysical view of the world. However you get it, you will tend to stop searching when you find it, and experience that joy.
5. When you do find the answer, embrace it for yourself only. It may be a universal truth, but it may not be universally applicable. This is the difference between the Course and traditional religions. Most traditional religions believe that

1

theirs is a universal truth that must be adopted by all (ie: their belief that it is universally applicable). The belief of the Course is that there are a thousand paths.

6. Remember to do what gives you joy. Every Bible printed is simply man's interpretation of God's word. If you feel joy embracing an all-loving God - do it! If you need a God capable of anger and vengeance - go for it! If you don't need any God for joy - that's OK! Simply remember that any of these beliefs has the power to determine your life.

Take the quiz that follows to test your beliefs. The questions may seem broad. The answers may therefore seem elusive. However, the quiz is designed to lead you to these answers in a quantified way:

1. With what types of beliefs will I have the greatest problems?
2. Who am I now in terms of my beliefs?
3. Do I have sufficient motivation to change my beliefs?
4. Is it worth my while to change my beliefs in order to decrease my pain and increase my joy?

This self quiz will help to give you an idea of your current belief system versus that of the Course. Simply take the quiz and then move on to the narrative that follows. Do not, after reading the narrative, change your responses! Your initial instinctive answers will be an important guide to your true feelings. These answers also will help you see any changes that might occur after you have spent some time in this material.

Completing the exhibits in this book

Exhibit 1a is the first of many "to-be-self-answered" exhibits directly related to the Course. Each is shown by an exhibit designation. For example, the first exhibit is 1a. For ease of reference, the number is its chapter number in this book. Thus, the exhibit appears in chapter one. The letter following the number is the alphabetical order of the appearance of that exhibit within the chapter. Thus, exhibit 1a is the first exhibit in chapter one. All exhibits are identified in this way. If you later want to find an exhibit, there is a directory of exhibits in the front of the book. This directory has the title and exhibit designation of all exhibits in this book.

Some of the exhibits in this book are referred to as "questionnaires", or are said to contain "questions". Many of these exhibits actually contain statements. You will be asked to respond to these statements, which is why they are referred to as questions. Much of the value of this book comes from your honest completion of these questionnaire exhibits. You do not need to share the results with anyone, so be honest with yourself. The results are designed to show you two critical aspects of your ability to get benefit from A Course in Miracles. The first is to become aware of those parts of your belief system which may block you from swapping pain for joy. Second, are your ways of solving problems as compared to Course ways.

These questionnaires are all designed so that you give your answer before seeing the Course answer. You will lose much of the benefit if you read ahead of the exhibit before completing it. The goal is for you to record your own feelings and beliefs. There is no "right" answer. The purpose is to understand what you currently believe. After you answer the questions, you can compare your answers to the Course answers. This will give you the additional benefit of seeing how different your beliefs are from those of the Course.

In some cases the blank "to be completed" questionnaires in the book may be copied. In each such case, it is clearly noted. You may copy them, if you wish, for your personal use–not in bulk or for resale. However, the rest of the book is copyrighted and cannot be copied without the publisher's permission.

Almost all such questionnaires, including 1a, are designed to be used with the same number evaluation system. This is a simple scale to reflect your feelings or beliefs by a numbered answer. One extreme is -10. This shows either strong disagreement with the idea or the most negative view of the idea. If you are neutral about the idea, simply answer with a 0. This shows that you have no feelings one way or the other. The other extreme is +10. This shows either strong agreement with the idea or the most positive view of the idea. Your answer to any question can be anywhere between -10 and +10. Thus there are 21 possible numbers, including 0, you can use to indicate the strength and direction of your feelings.

Not everyone's evaluation of which number to assign to their feelings will be the same. However, that doesn't make any real difference. It is far more important that each person answer each questionnaire consistently. Whatever he or she feels is the right number will, by definition, be right for them. There very well may be differences between people's answers if you are using this book in a group and comparing notes. The process of talking about those differences can in itself be productive.

Measuring your basic beliefs

The start will enable you to understand where your beliefs are today, versus the Course beliefs. Following is a questionnaire (1a) which you can answer with these -10 to +10 responses. This particular questionnaire (1a) can be copied, even though this book is copyrighted.

MEASURING YOUR BASIC BELIEFS
exhibit 1a

FILL THIS IN FOR YOURSELF

Answer each question by rating your belief system on a scale of from -10 to +10. Strong disagreement is -10. Strong agreement is +10. If you are neutral (neither agree nor disagree) use 0. Answer the questions without looking ahead in this book. The method of evaluating your answers is given immediately after this exhibit. Do not read it until you have answered all of the questions! If you have questions about how to complete this exhibit, reread page 3.

A. MOTIVATION

[   ] 1. It is to my benefit to change.
[   ] 2. There must be another (better) way.
[   ] 3. It hurts too much not to change.
[   ] 4. I am willing to do whatever is necessary.

_____ MOTIVATION TOTAL

B. SPIRITUAL FAITH

[   ] 1. I believe that there is little spiritually to help me in the knowledge of this world.
[   ] 2. Spiritual beliefs can affect worldly realities.
[   ] 3. Ruthless people may seem to prevail, but they pay too high a price.
[   ] 4. I believe that the answer is inside of me; no one else has it for me.

_____ SPIRITUAL FAITH TOTAL

C. FAITH IN MIND CONTROL

[   ] 1. My feeling that this world could be as dangerous as my belief system makes it.
[   ] 2. The strength of my agreement with the Course's position that from my perception flows my reality.
[   ] 3. My belief that tough minded people may suffer, while love minded people tend to have peace.
[   ] 4. The strength of my belief that the stuff of this world isn't worth thinking about, let alone having.

_____ MIND CONTROL TOTAL

_____ D. TOTAL OF ALL THREE SECTIONS

Course beliefs include a challenge in which our ego is in a constant tug of war with our Holy Spirit. The ego is what some people might call our dark side, the devil, our worst fears, etc. The Holy Spirit (HS) is a message within us, given to us by God, enabling us to relate to God. HS is in us even after we, by our decision, created our separation from God. The goal of the ego is to murder us. The goal of the HS is to bring us back into communion with God.

Since the belief of the Course is that we created our own separation from God, we are also in control of our rejoining God. This is different from the belief of most traditional religions: that our world was created by God to test us. The traditional reason for these tests is that God causes us to suffer (ie: Job in the Bible) so that we can be closer to Him/Her. The Course belief is that this separation is caused by choosing fear instead of love. He/She thinks that we are still back there with Him. We are, in effect, dreaming a nightmare of hell, called this world. We created it by our desire to be more powerful than God. We continue that power struggle, which gives rise to our hell.

Replacing pain with joy requires only replacing your ego messages with messages from HS. In order to do this you need to change your belief system. This has four requirements. These are your convictions that:

1. It is to my benefit to change.

The essence of this is that something in my life will be better if I change. For the traditional believer it is his belief that it will cause God to love him more than others. For the atheist, it is simply to achieve a better life in this world. For everybody else, it is some combination of these.

2. There must be another (better) way.

This issue is that whatever my way is now, it doesn't work. Life can't be this tough. There are people who, in my own observation, don't have these kinds of problems. I need to find that "secret."

3. It hurts too much not to change.

When the pain gets too intense, too lengthy or too repetitive, this person decides to change. The basic belief is that whatever the changed life is like it can't be as bad as this. In a worldly sense, immigrants who leave one culture and all they know and love for another unknown culture are an example of this.

4. I am willing to do whatever is necessary.

By the time a person reaches this conclusion, he either sinks into a shell of withdrawal, or sets out to find *any* solution. The withdrawn person is usually not heard from again. Those who find the Course are looking for a solution.

The reason these four beliefs are necessary is that the Course is simple, but it is not easy. These four beliefs give us the motivation that generates the energy to see it through.

Most of us have spent a lifetime developing a four-part belief system that must be overcome since it is the reverse of this:

1. I believe that there is help for me in the vast knowledge of this world.

We tend to grow up with a strong indoctrination in the value of the "vast knowledge" of this world. This is a basic belief in man's ability to solve his own problems with little spiritual resource. From our perception, looking at our tiny space in the universe through a microscope, this certainly appears to be the case. When we trade the microscope for a telescope, our view might change. If you are rooted in a worldly solution, the Course is not for you.

2. God will get me on the right path. He is watching me.

Most traditional believers operate on the idea that God is without, not within. Therefore, if I pray, He will come to my rescue. These can be the folks who have little spiritual faith (ie: agnostics). Or they may, in our society, seem to embrace all of the outward symbols of the Judo-Christian ethic. There is no necessary correlation between spiritual belief and joy. It can be hard to sort them out since there are atheists with more integrity and joy than the most devout of traditional believers and vice versa. This can be summed up by a sonnet from the Course:

"I am responsible for what I see. I choose the feelings I experience and I decide upon the goal I would achieve and everything that seems to happen to me I ask for, and receive as I have asked."　　(A Course in Miracles - text P. 418)

3. Ruthless people may seem to prevail, but they pay too high a price.

The belief in ruthlessness is a symptom of a problem belief system. Being ruthless is usually a cover for dependency and low self-esteem. This person believes that the tough or ruthless person has the answer that has evaded him. This belief is that in this world one needs to be ruthless to survive. This mistakes ruthlessness for what the Course describes as a more appropriate answer to a "call for love." The ruthless person simply substitutes his own rationalizations and low self esteem for loving solutions. Thus, a truism of this world: "power corrupts."

4. I know the answer is inside of me, no else has it for me.

The opposite of this, "the answer is out there–somewhere", is a common problem. It has given rise to innumerable idols, belief systems, therapies, gurus and cults. Outside beliefs can be the lazy way out. The answer is not in: 1) a fearless leader, 2) the Bible, the Koran or A Course in Miracles, 3) a great new therapy or therapist, or 4) anyone or anything else. It is in you. The message of the greatest writings depends on your interpretation of them. Hitler used the Bible to justify killing the Jews. The Middle East has endless "holy wars." What country has gone to war without God on its side? The extreme of this is to give up your own power. Those who do give up their own power depend on something or someone else and therefore have no power. A common example of giving up your power to someone and something else is this: "the Bible, as interpreted by some priest, minister or rabbi, has all of the answers." All religious beliefs have a spiritual basis which brings people closer to God and to peace. It is departure from that spiritual bedrock that causes trouble.

The Course would respond to each of these four points in the same order, as follows:

1. This world is as dangerous as your belief system makes it.

A strong tenant of the Course is that everyone else we encounter is but a mirror of our beliefs. Thus, the fundamental thrust of the Course: from your perception flows your reality. This is said in many different ways in the Course. Perhaps more than any other Course belief, this can be difficult for people. It is important to note that this is not a belief in giving up any defense. It is simply that the defenses change to viable ones; those of our inherent spiritual power: "If I defend myself, I am attacked."

    2. The Course's position is that our beliefs make our world realities. As Abraham Lincoln said, "Folks are about as happy as they make up their minds to be."

Now reread the comment to #1, beginning on the previous page.

3. Tough minded people suffer and die young.

Love minded people know the difference between love and a call for love and how to answer both. A call for love, in Course terms, is any action other than love. Love does not mean being a door mat. In the Course, intention can be very important. Don't look at what the person did, look at the gift in his doing it. The most seemingly selfless acts, if done for the wrong reasons, have both negative and positive value. For example, giving to charity to look good results in negative energy for the giver but benefit to the charity. Conversely, the most destructive acts have some good.

    4. The stuff of this world is not worth thinking about, let alone having. Have the joy the Course offers and everything else you need will flow.

This does not mean that if you adopt the Course, you will have wealth or be rich. It does mean that if you follow the Course, what you have will match what you need.

Total your score by adding the number rating of each answer and putting the total, by category, in the space provided. You can find the areas where you need the most change by then comparing the total of each score in each of the three categories. If you scored under 5 for any answer or under 20 for any of the three totals, this is an area that needs work. Of course, the lower your score is, the more change in belief you will need in that category.

For example, if you have low motivation (Section A), it will be difficult for you to take the time, energy and pain necessary to look at your life as the Course does. Similarly, you may have very high motivation, but simply have too much faith in this world (Spiritual faith, Section B) to benefit from the Course's highly spiritual approach.

Finally, you may have great motivation and great faith in spiritual solutions, but great resistance to the idea that your mind can control your life (faith in mind control, Section C). If this is the case, you may want to find an approach other than the Course. The Course is basically a course in mind control.

How low, or high, need the results be to make these decisions? There is no fixed answer. You may find that your numerical results vary widely in each of these three sections. For example, if you have high scores in sections A (Motivation) and C (Mind control), but low results in Section B (Spiritual faith) you might have a lot of inner turmoil about the Course. In this case you would have both the push (motivation) and the pull (faith in mind control). However, you would have great difficulty in letting go of your belief in solutions arising out of this world.

This illustrates another important use of these scores. The gap, or differences, between the scores in any section can be just as telling as the absolute results. One further illustration may help. To do this test, use average scores. The average is simply the total by section divided by 4. Thus, if a section total is 32, the average is 8. If, for example you scored an average of 8 each in any two sections, but an average of 3 in a third section, you could still have problems in using the Course to change your life.

However, as the Course says, every problem is a gift. By finding your areas of greatest resistance you can concentrate on them. This will help you to pinpoint the area(s) of your belief system that need work, enabling the Course to help you. Conversely, it can show you what your belief system is and therefore help you in finding some other alternative or path to that help.

Since this is a guide to using the Course, let's turn back to using these results for that purpose. The reason big gaps in these scores can be a problem is that motivation, worldly faith, mind control faith are the three most critical beliefs in successfully carrying out the message of the Course.

The Course is simple, but it is not easy. Without a high motivation you will probably founder. The Course is a spiritual belief system. If you are trapped in a high degree of belief in the ability of the stuff of this world to solve your problems and give you joy, that is the opposite of a spiritual belief. Remember, this is a course in mind training. If you strongly disagree with the idea of mind training, you probably won't get the results you want from the Course.

However, even if you have a big gap, all is not yet lost. Look at the specific answers in your weakest or lowest scoring section. To illustrate, we can take one section and look at it in detail. The motivation section (A) for most people will tend to be strong, or they probably would not be reading this book.

The two areas where most people tend to have problems with the Course are faith in: 1. spiritual beliefs (Section B) and, 2. in mind control (Section C). To select one of these sections as our example, we probably should pick the most difficult. For many people, that will tend to be mind control. Many people tend to have a problem with the Course's description of the extensive ability of our belief system to control our lives. The Course repeats, in myriad ways, a basic theme. That theme is that the world and your fellow man is but a mirror of your perceptions.

To illustrate, question C1 is a stopper for most people:

1. "My feeling is that this world could be as dangerous as my belief system makes it."

As they think about the broad extent of their fears, many people tend to believe secretly that they have so many fears that if the world really reflected all of their fears, it would be hell. The Course, for many people, answers that it is! This illustrates a basic belief of the Course that we created this world. It reflects our belief in our separation from God. From this it follows that the insanity of this world cannot be of God. Otherwise God is indeed angry and hostile, having created this hell for us.

Question C2 is another, milder, way of addressing the same issue. Many people's answer to this question will tend to reflect less belief in C2 than in C1. This is understandable in looking again at C2:

2. "The strength of my agreement with the Course's position that from my perception flows my reality."

This concept is foreign to the way we tend to be brought up. We tend to learn as children that our reality, or our "life or work" as it is most commonly stated, is created by hard work, perseverance, cooperation, education, etc. Conversely, the Course simply says that these attributes are but results themselves of our belief system. We engage in hard work versus "the easy life" because of our belief system in one or the other. That belief system gives us our perceptions about what works. From our belief system flows our perceptions of the world. These perceptions determine how we act and how we act creates our reality.

If we believe that our friend (or mother, father, brother, sister) is a holy, loving child of God (HLCG), our perception of that person's behavior toward us will be markedly different than if we believe he is an SOB. He may be a murder-thief-rapist, but the Course says that if we see him as a child of God, he will probably not steal from, murder or rape us. Many people have a real problem with this idea. It is too early in this work to solve that conflict now. Suffice to say that this is not a course in turning the other cheek.

Question C3 is another variation on this basic theme:

3. "My belief that tough minded people may suffer, while love minded people tend to have peace."

There is an apparent error in this question. It is the broad difference in what we each mean by "love minded" and "tough minded." The closer you are to Course principles the more you will tend to see "tough minded" differently, and the higher your score will be. As you move closer to Course principles, your spiritual view will create your mind's ability to control your reality. The more you see the person you are here in this world, as removed from God, the more you see the need for traditional "toughness" as opposed to "love" mindedness. In short, the further you are from God the more you see two types of: people, belief systems, minds, etc.

The last question, C4, brings us to the real difference between your beliefs and those of the Course. There are many people in, and out of, metaphysics who have a materialistic view of mind training. They are going to use metaphysics to manifest something: a new car, house, spouse, money, etc. Nothing could be farther from the Course's position. The Course simply holds that since we, not God, elected to be here, how can God know or care if we are driving the particular fancy luxury car of our dreams?

Question C4 is intended to bring out this belief, no matter how latent:

4. "The strength of my belief that the stuff of this world isn't worth thinking about, let alone having."

So, if mind training isn't good for manifesting a pot of money, what is it good for? The Course says it is for your atonement with God. The Course tells us that God doesn't even hear our manifestation requests that don't further this atonement goal. You created the separation. He wants you back. You have to get back yourself, or at least have a little willingness to do it.

Therefore, even if you believe in mind control, it will not do you as much good if you don't believe in using it for atonement. If you are going to manifest a castle on the Rhine, the Course will not work. It is meant for a spiritual castle. Reflecting the experience of thousands of people, the Course does work in building that castle.

Chapter 2

Why Does it Hurt?

The Course says that what hurts us is ourselves. The result is that the world we experience is a mirror of our beliefs and feelings. Therefore, what we see is what we get. This means that our experiences arise out of our beliefs and feelings about ourselves. The Course sums it up in Lesson 32, "I have invented the world I see." So, the evil, pain, problems, arguments, anger, fights, jealousies, etc. we experience are all created in our heads. At this point, based on this comment alone, we may lose a number of readers. The rewards, for those of you who stay with it, are more than worth it.

Your life mirrors your beliefs

First, let's look at the ways in which you resist this "mirroring" idea in your life. Few of us, when faced with a "difficult" person, believe that our being upset with that person results from our own negative self image. However, as the Course says in Lesson 34, "I could see peace instead of this."

That means that what you see is what you get. Whatever your investment is in an outcome different from the one that "difficult" person is proposing or creating, let it go. The Course goes one step further and tells you to look for the gift from that "difficult" person. If you are still resisting these Course ideas–great! You now can look, in an organized way, at the reasons for that resistance. This will give you more insight for either stopping or continuing this quest. Following is exhibit 2a where you to enter your feelings as they are now. Your feelings can be the windows to your beliefs. Therefore, if you work on your cherished feelings you can use that work to change your beliefs.

The difference between the last exhibit (1a) and this exhibit (2a) is that 1a asks about your beliefs and 2a asks about your feelings. If you had problems answering 1a, this is a second chance. You will recall that in exhibit 1a we looked at motivation and spiritual and mind control beliefs. In 2a we are looking at the results that flow from those beliefs.

If your fears are a +10, it really doesn't make much difference what your fear is about. That fear is crippling. I will illustrate this in my own case. I grew up with a crippling fear that if anyone "discovered" that my father was Jewish I would be murdered. That fear controlled my life so much that my behavior resulted from it. That fear arose out of my childhood experiences in Catholic and "Christian" boarding schools. The experience of beatings and sexual molestation because of my Jewish father was so severe that there was no doubt in my mind about my belief. Yet, this fear was my choice. I could have seen it differently.

What led to my ultimate freedom were my high levels of motivation, faith and, eventually, belief in mind control, all of which are shown in exhibit 1a. However, during the years I held this belief my anger levels were very high. The level of my anger was therefore the barometer of my inner conflict. The Course is clear about this. It says in many ways that fear gives rise to anger. How we see ourselves (ie: as in my case, a to-be-murdered Jew) is how we see others. If I believed myself to be a target for murder, then I must believe that others are murderers. If others are murderers then so am I. This is what the Course describes as the classic ego state. The ultimate goal of our own ego is to murder us. In this way I let my ego control my life.

If you have a strong tendency to either withdraw or to fight (ie: +6 or above) you are functioning at what the Course calls an ego level. You will not want to either withdraw or fight if you believe yourself and others to be holy, loving children of God (HLCG). Your sense of superiority or inferiority, which is the same thing in the Course philosophy, is the final indicator of to which voice (ego or HS) you are listening. The Course view is that there can be no such idea as superiority if you are a HLCG.

Now, give exhibit 2a a try. Do not "peek ahead" before completing at least columns a and b of this exhibit. If you can't answer columns c and d now, come back to them later. If you have questions about using the -10 to 0 to +10 ranking system, refer to the detailed explanation in Chapter 1.

**MY FEELINGS AS A GUIDE IN APPLYING
COURSE IN MIRACLES BELIEFS**
exhibit 2a

Use the same ranking system about your feelings in other exhibits. Only column c calls for a narrative answer. The ranking system for the other three columns is from -10 (strongly negative) to 0 (neither agree nor disagree) to +10 (strongly positive). If you can't respond to columns c and d now, leave them and do them later.

Belief / Feeling	Strength Of		c) What is the lesson from A Course in Miracles? (leave blank if unknown)	d) This applies to me
	a) my feeling	b) need change		
My Fears Control Me				
Strong Anger Results				
So I Tend to Be Closed				
So I Fight or Hide				
And Need to Be Superior				

A Course in Miracles in 5 Minutes

The Course says there are two contrasting emotions, fear versus love. So, let's start with fear. If you have a high level of fear about the world, you have identified a threshold problem. Fear is not only paralyzing in this world, it also impedes your ability to receive any spiritual gifts. It is difficult to see yourself as a holy, loving child of God while you are terrified into inaction.

Do you know why fear overcomes you? It is almost always a belief system on your part, mostly arising from childhood messages. The most common example of this is if you do "X", then "Y" will happen. The "X" may be to fall in love, not fall in love, too much or not enough sex, over eat, under eat, work too hard or not work hard enough. These warnings come in a bewildering array of possibilities. They are limited only by the well-intended madness of our parents, siblings and authority figures.

The "Y," or what can happen, is similarly insane. It ranges from going blind (masturbation) to warts (scab picking) to death from AIDS, which results from having "illegal" sex. All of this ends when you make three decisions. The first decision is that God is loving, not vengeful. There is not one vengeful bone in His body, to mix metaphors.

The Course has only one answer

The second decision is that you are a holy, loving child of that loving God. The third decision is that everyone else is, too. When you have those three beliefs, your entire life will change. Since this is a course in mind control, its sole purpose is to bring you to those three beliefs.

Now, watch what happens to the rest of the questions in the lefthand column, as you embrace these beliefs. You can't: oppose, have anger, withdraw, fight or feel superior, if you believe that you and everyone else are all holy, loving children of a loving God.

There are two problems with this, both arising out of this world. First, most of us have been taught that either God doesn't exist (about 5%) or more commonly, that He/She is vengeful (about 95%). The basis for His anger or vengefulness is no less an authority than the Bible. He has "smitten" and "smoted" seemingly endless people who "sinned." This is not the Course's belief. In the Course's view, this is merely a human interpretation of what God must be like.

A famous quotation is that "God made man in his image and man returned the favor." A result of man creating God in man's image is something like this: "Since we are capable of anger so God must be too." The Course, on the other hand, tells us clearly that God is a God of love, and His anger is man's way of making Him like us, instead of making us like Him.

This gives rise to the second of the two problems. This is our fear that if we behave with this "love," particularly to our enemies, we will be crushed. It is this difference between the Course God and the angry God of traditional religions that makes the Course unique. It promises that this will not happen, for three reasons. First, your enemies will disappear. Second, you will learn to distinguish between what the Course calls love versus a call for love. Third, once you can distinguish between them you will know how to react in a way that will always work.

As you can see, the reason your fears dissolve is the same for each of these questions. Your belief system changes. How to accomplish that change is the message of the Course. Keep your responses to these questions. If you go forward and work the Course, you will be astonished to see how different your answers will become. It works!

To illustrate, following is exhibit 2b which is 2a with my own pre-Course belief system inserted into it.

MY FEELINGS AS A GUIDE IN APPLYING
COURSE IN MIRACLES BELIEFS
exhibit 2b

Use the same ranking system about your feelings as is used in other exhibits. Only column c calls for a narrative answer. The ranking system for the other three columns is from -10 (strongly negative) to 0 (neither agree nor disagree) to +10 (strongly positive). If you can't respond to columns c and d now, leave them and do them later.

Question / Feeling	Strength Of		c) What is the lesson from A Course in Miracles? (leave blank if unknown)	d) This applies to me
	a) my feeling	b) need change		
My Fears Control Me	+9	+9	*I am an HLCG.*	+10
Strong Anger Results	+9	+9	*I can only be angry at myself.*	+10
So I Tend to Be Closed	+8	+8	*I need not withdraw if others are HLCG.*	+10
So I Fight or Hide	+8	+8	*What is there to fight about - it only separates me from God.*	+10
And Need to Be Superior	+8	+8	*Now I know that as an HLCG I don't need to prove anything.*	+10

Notice how simple the Course answers are to the strong issues that controlled my life. You can achieve these results. Just stick with this book.

The Course versus motivation systems

There are many motivational schools, beliefs and trainings. The principal difference between them is their degree of spiritual belief. The Course is entirely spiritually based. Most motivation systems have as a goal achieving something of this world. The belief system of the Course is that there is nothing in or of this world worth having. Therefore, the sole goal of the Course is to achieve atonement, or a reuniting with God. What could be less worldly?

Many people who embark on the Course are refugees, from various worldly based motivational systems which did not work, or they would not be in the Course. To illustrate, the "triumph of Capitalism" resulting from the fall of Russia might lead one to believe that the ideas of this world are powerful. After all, isn't it the Capitalistic system with its great rewards that prevailed over a system of totalitarian economics? The Course answer to this question illustrates how radical the Course view is. The Course answer to this question is that it isn't a question. If it has to do with this world as opposed to God it is not answerable by God.

Whether we are Communist, capitalist, Republican, Democrat, male, female, straight, gay, Catholic, Moslem, black, white, blue or yellow is not within His perception. He only cares that we reunite with Him. Since, in the Course view, we made this nightmare called this world, we need to unmake it. Our power to do this is unlimited. Only our mind, being our belief system, prevents it.

The closest worldly motivational system to the Course is perhaps best expressed by Norman Cousins in two of his books: "Anatomy of an Illness" and "Head First, The Biology of hope". In these books, Cousins describes his own reaction versus those of others to cancer. These differences resulted from their differing beliefs. If you have any doubt about the infinite ability of the mind to control your life, read either of these two books. In "Head First", Cousins, then on the staff of the UCLA Hospital cancer treatment center, documents many patients' results, based on their beliefs. His work is not only inspiring, but more importantly, shows how a positive mental attitude resulted in miraculous recoveries.

Low self esteem - the curse of this planet

It may be helpful, in order to evaluate your current belief system, to look at it in a few more ways. Your self esteem flows from your beliefs. These are illustrated compared with the principles of the Course in exhibit 2c. This should help to show you where you are currently and what you need to do, according to the Course, to improve your self esteem.

Self esteem, in Course terms, is the result of your belief system. You cannot believe that you are a holy, loving child of God and have low self esteem. Again, to change your self esteem you need to have high motivation. Your self esteem will improve as you get rid of your anger. You can't be both angry and believe in a loving God. This then is another way of trying to understand the blocks to your peace.

One of the most difficult questions in this world is how to improve that self esteem. A measure of our view of ourself as a HLCG is given to us by the reflection in the world of our self esteem. Exhibit 2c shows the components of doing this. Your instinctive response is probably best. If you can't give an instinctive response, then do the next exhibit (2d) before answering the anger versus joy line. However, you should answer everything else in the exhibit 2c before going to the detailed anger versus joy exhibit, shown as exhibit 2d. Again, any questions about using the -10 to 0 to +10 ranking system are answered at the beginning of Chapter 1.

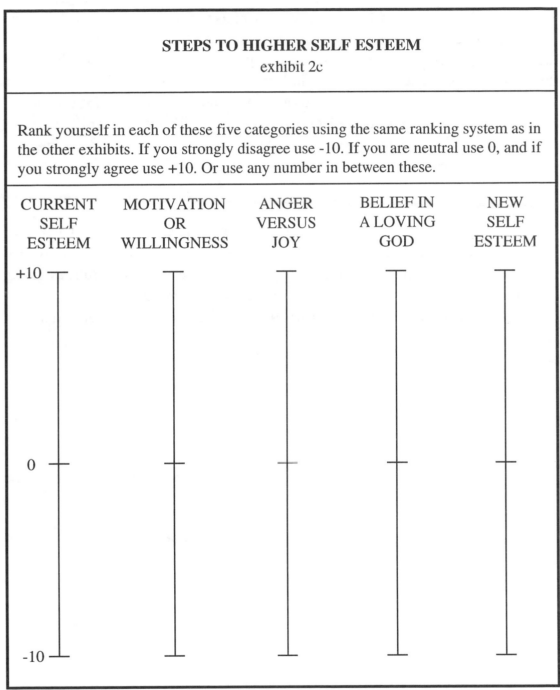

STEPS TO HIGHER SELF ESTEEM
exhibit 2c

Rank yourself in each of these five categories using the same ranking system as in the other exhibits. If you strongly disagree use -10. If you are neutral use 0, and if you strongly agree use +10. Or use any number in between these.

CURRENT SELF ESTEEM	MOTIVATION OR WILLINGNESS	ANGER VERSUS JOY	BELIEF IN A LOVING GOD	NEW SELF ESTEEM

A Course in Miracles in 5 Minutes

As you plot your own belief system for each of these five measures, remember that for this purpose, there is no absolute definition of what +10 and -10 means. Only your definition is important. However, to be sure that you are being fair to yourself, be certain that you apply the same standard to each.

For example, you will measure your level of commitment in the Motivation line. Apply this same standard to the Belief in a loving God line. If you apply a different scale or standard to the Motivation line than to the line on Belief in a loving God, you may not benefit from the exercise. You know your own belief system. You understand the depth of your feelings. This is not a time to fool yourself.

Perhaps the most difficult of these to analyze is the anger versus joy line. We may know how motivated we are. We generally know where we are in our spiritual beliefs, and we usually have a fairly good idea of our own self esteem. Most people understand that low self esteem is the curse of this planet. However, we can have difficulty assessing our anger versus joy, since that is loaded with personal judgment.

Exhibit 2d may help you address each part of anger versus joy. Place yourself in each part.

YOUR VIEW OF THE WORLD
(another way of looking at anger versus joy)
exhibit 2d

Use the same -10 to 0 to +10 ranking to show where you are on the spectrum of each of the first three questions. Then average your numerical answers to place yourself on the final Anger versus joy line. A detailed explanation for the -10 to +10 evaluation system is given at the start of Chapter 1.

MY WORLD IS:

OPPRESSIVE   KIND

-10   0   +10

MOST PEOPLE ARE:

ATTACKING   GOD'S CHILDREN

-10   0   +10

WHEN "ATTACKED", I:

AM INDIGNANT   SEE THE GIFT

-10   0   +10

MY FINAL ANGER VERSUS JOY IS:
(average the three above)

ANGER   JOY

-10   0   +10

A Course in Miracles in 5 Minutes

It may help to take a look at this in another way. The exhibit that follows uses some common views of our brothers and sisters. These illustrate where we are today and how the Course addresses these feelings. Based on your current beliefs, either in the principles of the Course or not, fill in your answers under "Course message" and "positive gift." The answer must be how you feel. You don't have to show it to anyone else, but do be true to yourself. If you don't know, just guess, and if you can't guess, fill in your most instinctive immediate reaction.

Examples of your own answers could be: "I want to kill him" or, "I try to think about something else" or, "I get real mad" or, "I am so sad that I want to cry." Examples of your own guess as to a positive gift from this feeling are: "It reminds me that I need to work on this." or, "Are you kidding, there is nothing positive about feeling this way." or, "I suppose that it could be _____."

There are no right or wrong answers. The sole purpose is to note your feelings so that you can compare them to the answers from the Course. To get real value from this do not skip ahead, beyond exhibit 2e on the opposite page.

HOW MY PERCEPTION FLOWS FROM MY SELF IMAGE exhibit 2e		
FEELING	COURSE ANSWER (or my own answer)	POSITIVE GIFT (or my guess)
When I think that someone doesn't like me.		
When someone is better looking than I am.		
When I think that someone has more education than me.		
When I think that I am not as smart as someone else.		
When I am jealous because someone has more money than me.		

A Course in Miracles in 5 Minutes

What does this prove? All it does is to show you where you currently are in your own feelings about other people. In worldly terms, it is a measure of self-esteem, which is your perception of yourself. In Course terms it is far more telling. Self esteem is, in Course terms, a highly accurate measure of your perception of the world. You cannot accept anyone else until you accept yourself. This includes your and others' love, sexuality, personality, appearance, interests, accomplishments, motivations, joy, anger, hostility and fear.

Exhibit 2e is one more step toward knowing yourself. If you can identify these aspects of yourself you are on the first leg of accepting them. If you cannot identify them, even in the privacy of your own thoughts, you may not be at a level where the Course, or anything like it, can be helpful. You are in what the psychologists call "denial." Identifying them doesn't mean being happy with them; it means being able to deal with them.

Once you can accept who you really are, you can begin to accept others as they really are. The problem with this, in Course terms, is that if you are an angry, hostile, fearful, mean, SOB, that is how you will see everybody and everything else. The Course is clear that your world is merely a reflection of your beliefs about yourself. Whether you accept your beliefs doesn't change this "law," which is basic in the Course. However, recognizing your beliefs enables you to deal with them.

The Course tells us that what we believe creates our world. This means that from our perception flows our reality. So, if we don't like our reality, all we have to do is to change our perception of it. This is a staggering thought, so much so that at this stage we may lose many of our readers. They will ask themselves this self serving question: "Do you mean to say that if I am in (some incredibly difficult situation) that I can get out of it by changing my mind?" This is self serving, because the Course doesn't say you will always get out of it. It says that sometimes you won't get into it. That thought is simply too painful for many people.

To illustrate how this works, use exhibit 2e, which you just completed, and redo it with Course ideas. This is shown in exhibit 2f.

HOW MY PERCEPTION
FLOWS FROM MY SELF IMAGE
exhibit 2f

FEELING	COURSE ANSWER (or my own answer)	POSITIVE GIFT (or my guess)
When I think that someone doesn't like me.	I remember that this is my perception only, flowing from my own feelings about myself.	I am thankful for this reminder of who I really am, no matter how painful.
When someone is better looking than I am.	THE COURSE ANSWER IS ALWAYS THE SAME	
When I think that someone has more education than me.	THE COURSE ANSWER IS ALWAYS THE SAME	
When I think that I am not as smart as someone else.	THE COURSE ANSWER IS ALWAYS THE SAME	
When I am jealous because someone has more money than me.	THE COURSE ANSWER IS ALWAYS THE SAME	

A Course in Miracles in 5 Minutes

Crazy? Like a fox! What are the issues in exhibit 2f? They are: social acceptance, appearance, education, intelligence and money. These are the stuff of this world. The Course says that to the extent that you give these issues importance, they will become important to you, even though they have no real value. You may be asking yourself how you can get along in this world by disregarding them. The answer from the Course is that you don't need to worry about them. Most people have these worldly issues greatly enlarged in importance. If you enlarge these issues, it is always at the expense of who you and others really are as holy, loving children of God. When you believe that you are both HLCG, other issues become more important.

What are the other issues? They are first, yourself and your self-perception. To put it together, suppose you were unemployed (or single, yearning for a mate). Picture yourself with someone who has the intelligence of Albert Einstein. This person has been reincarnated to look like the most handsome or beautiful person imaginable. He/She came with an unlimited bank account and this person hated you. He/She can only hurt you if you need their approval or money. You don't need anything from him/her. You don't even need the job that person might offer you.

How can this be? First, you are employed by God, so you don't need that person's job or approval. Second, you know yourself to be a holy, loving child of God. It is not their approval you seek, but your own. Third, you know that as a HLCG, there will be few who will reject you. Finally, those few who do are presenting you with a marvelous gift. That gift is their getting out of your life, so you can get on with being a HLCG. You have no need to seek out or yearn for their approval. Your only need approval from yourself and God.

Chapter 3

When it Hurts

In Course terms, the outside world you experience is the world you have created by your inner beliefs. Negative beliefs cause personal pain. Since your pain is a direct result of your belief system, it follows that you will hurt when:

1. You are alone
2. You are with people
3. You are awake
4. You are asleep

This is a lot of pain, which you cannot escape. Isn't it worth doing something about? Since you carry it with you, the only thing you can do about it is to change yourself. This is simple, but again, it is not easy. The Course has worked for countless people; perhaps it can work for you as well.

The inner conflict

If you feel negative about yourself you will try to overcompensate. You will do this in one or both of the following ways:

1. Trying to be perfect, although you never can be perfect enough to compensate for your self-negativism.

2. Trying to please people so that they "won't hurt you".

Notice the conflict here. You want to be perfect, but at the same time you are trying to please others. This means you are trying to conform to someone else's idea of what perfection is. The problem with this is that everyone has a different idea about what perfection means. So you are caught in an endless quest for the impossible. What frustration!

Of course, you will be hurt by others because you are so fragile. You have no way to avoid the hurt since you have no spiritual belief system of your own. In your endless quest for perfection, you will rocket from one person or guru to another, seeking to fulfill their fantasies of what perfection is. In biblical terms this would be called "idolatry." The Course simply says that who you are is a matter for you and God only. So keep it between the two of you.

In short, you do not need gurus, therapists, priests, ministers or rabbis. Any of these people can be helpful, but you don't need them. You can reach this goal by yourself, and waiting for the perfect person to help you can just be procrastinating. After some period of time looking for Mr. or Ms. "Wonderful", you will perceive that the person is you. That is a basic message of the Course.

When you begin to believe that it is you who are the perfect, holy, loving child of God, your inner conflict will decrease. At this point, you will begin to value yourself and your serenity. Following is an exhibit for you to fill in. The purpose of exhibit 3a, "How I Seek Myself in Others", is to help you see how far along this road to non-idolatry you are.

Again, don't peek ahead. Your major benefit will come from just filling in the information for yourself, based on your instinctive reactions. You are not trying to achieve any preconceived standard or answer. You are trying to figure out your true feelings about yourself.

HOW I SEEK MYSELF IN OTHERS
exhibit 3a

Answer in any written narrative that clearly states your feelings. Try to answer without looking ahead.

When I don't find peace and acceptance in myself, I:

I look for acceptance in this way because without it, I:

The only way I can change this is to:

If you have difficulty in completing this - *do not look ahead!* Here are a few tips. When you don't find peace and acceptance within yourself, it generally means that you believe that somehow you are going to find it with, through or in someone else. The Course calls that a "magic" belief or "special" relationship. Your subconscious belief is that someone–boss, lover, friend, guru, lawyer, teacher, doctor, therapist, consultant or employee–has the magic solution that has evaded you.

As you read this, you may be angry or amused at your silliness in giving someone else this much power. You also may think that since we get lots of information from others from kindergarten on, it seems quite normal to be looking for this "information" from outside yourself.

The Course answers that it is not "information." It is belief. Would it help you to get all of the information possible about the safety of ham, if a devout Jew, or eating meat on Fridays, if a devout Catholic in certain countries, or eating during Ramadan, if a Moslem? Obviously not! It is your religious, parental and historical messages, making a belief system, which cause you to have these eating habits. You might sneak in a little of the "forbidden fruit," but you would not be at peace if you did so.

At least as such a devout person you would know what your "forbidden fruit" or act was that violated their belief system. However, any difficulty in completing exhibit 3a may reflect a more confused belief system. You may, for example, not even know what your "forbidden fruit" is. Worse than this, you may not even have an identifiable belief system.

Our beliefs cause our conflicts

For example, would you rather believe that to appease the gods and be happy, you need to not kill any animals or, on the other hand, that you need to kill one rabbit: 1. each day, or 2. only when things go wrong or 3. only on certain God appeasing days? Perhaps you might believe that you were: 4: not killing enough, or killing too many, rabbits each day, or 5. not killing them in the "right" way or 6. not killing the right kinds of rabbits.

Finally, you might decide that killing rabbits doesn't appease the gods. Therefore, your killing is only depleting the rabbit population, making you further depressed and soiling your clothes. At this point you might decide to switch from rabbits to cats (asking forgiveness from cat lovers). If you were to do this, you would be faced with the same six questions, only now about cats. Or you might decide not to kill anything.

If you reached this point you might then believe that: 1. killing animals to appease the gods is dumb, or 2. you will worship the animal instead of killing it, or 3. you will switch from animals to insects, birds, reptiles, humans, flowers, trees, shrubbery, followers or leaders or 4. you will build monuments to the gods, or 5. you will do incantations, or 6. you will do good deeds, or 7. you will be "nice" to a certain group, or to all, people, or . . . it is endless.

At some point, many rabbits, cats, insects, birds, reptiles, humans, flowers, trees, shrubbery, leaders, followers, monuments, incantations or deeds later, you may feel that you still are not at peace. This is when you are ready to start your inner journey. This is what the Course in Miracles is about.

Completing exhibit 3a can tell you how many "things" you have sacrificed, and can bring you closer to looking at the root cause. It is you! You need only change your thinking, that is, your belief system. This is a Course in mind training. So, stop at this point, go back to exhibit 3a again and try to complete it. If you go beyond this point without a good try at completing it, you have done yourself a disservice.

Now, let's see how exhibit 3a might look if filled out by someone who is at the rabbit killing stage. This person believes that the answer is "out there".

HOW I SEEK MYSELF IN OTHERS
a non-Course view
exhibit 3b

When I don't find peace and acceptance in myself, I:

...try to achieve it by getting acceptance from others. To get this acceptance I will do almost anything. My need for validation is so desperate that I will kill rabbits, build monuments, or do anything that I think will please others. At some point I realize that they don't know any more than I do. I then try to find someone who does. I keep repeating this.

I look for acceptance in this way because without it, I:

...do not feel that I have value since none comes from inside me. I do this because I do not know who I am, since I can only see myself as others see me. In yielding this power to others I do not have to do the work in figuring out who I am. It is generally inconceivable to me that I could have the answers inside of me. I can never remember believing this, since I have been told ever since I can remember that I (fill in) 1. wasn't very smart, or 2. didn't have this kind of information, or 3. should look to the knowledge of the world to solve my problems.

The only way I can change this is to realize:

...that I can't kill enough rabbits to solve this problem. That it is possible that I may have value as a perfect, holy, loving child of God. If so, all of the "data" that I need is inside of me. To unlock it and use it, I need to believe that I am worthwhile, independent of what other people may think. If I am going to believe that I need to resolve my feeling of separation from God. This means that I created my own separation from God by my belief in it.
Therefore, to change it, all that I have to do is to change this belief. To change this belief, I need to know what must be undone in my present belief system and with what I need to replace it. I now know that it must be a belief that gives me value as a person.

The road to peace

The conclusions, in the last section of this exhibit, will now start this person on the road to peace. The journey can be a difficult one depending on how far he/she has to travel. The point is that it is a destination that can be reached. Exhibit 3c would be filled in by someone who has taken this journey.

HOW I SEEK MYSELF
a Course in Miracles view
exhibit 3c

When I don't find peace and acceptance in myself, I:

...go inside and ask the Holy Spirit to remind me that I am a holy, loving child of God and that, as such, there is nothing or no one who can disturb my peace. I know that when I have trouble doing this I need to reinforce my belief that as a child of God, I need only reduce the separation from Him that I feel in order to bring Him closer into my life.

I look for acceptance in this way because without it, I:

...would find myself again wandering all over the ways of this world to find peace, none of which work. I have taken that journey before. It has never led to a destination that resulted in anything but temporary peace. Even this temporary peace just caused more pain later, because it led me to the mistaken conclusion that something of this world could give me any lasting peace.

The only way I can change this is to:

...experience the quality of the peace that I achieve in this way and to continue to have the willingness to reduce the separation from God as much as possible.

"Achievement versus spirituality"

In the Western world, we tend to substitute "achievements" or "results" for inner peace: "He went to Harvard . . . Yale . . . has a PhD . . . is a doctor . . . company president . . . made a million dollars." Any of which are fine worldly statements about the person, but they don't say anything about his joy and/or peace. As we all know, many of these highly accomplished people are the most miserable SOBs, to themselves, their families and to everyone else.

In short, in our ultra-sophisticated Western society, we know better than to kill rabbits to appease the gods. Many people have simply decided that if there is a God, it is money. God wants them to be rich! That is their manifest destiny and their absolution. If there isn't a God, what difference does it make? So, they may as well do all they can to be rich and enjoy this life. Thus, our "spiritual" slogans tend to be, "He who dies with the most toys wins" or, "I have been rich and poor; rich is better." These types of testimonials to wealth are endless.

This course in mind training can change your perception of all of that, and in doing so, can bring you security and joy beyond anything you have experienced. Begin by listing your beliefs about yourself and your achievements in exhibit 3d on the following page.

MY BELIEFS AS AN ACHIEVEMENT STRIVER
exhibit 3d

Since I believe that I am not acceptable as I am, I can become acceptable by:

I believe that I need to do this because:

If I don't accomplish these goals, I will:

Do not continue until you have completed exhibit 3d! If you have not done so, go back and re-attempt it. Much of the benefit of this book comes from understanding your current belief system and comparing it to what the Course says it can be. This is one way of seeing if the Course makes sense for you.

People with this "Achievement Striving" view of life tend to respond as shown in exhibit 3e.

MY WORLDLY BELIEFS AS AN ACHIEVEMENT STRIVER
exhibit 3e

Since I believe that I am not acceptable as I am, I can become acceptable by:

...reaching levels of money and power attained only by few people. I can then substitute my achievements for who I really am, as a person. There is no effort or level to which I will not go to reach these achievements. For example, if I successfully "skirt" the law I will be even more acceptable and admired because I have done things that are dared by few people.

I believe that I need to do this because:

...I have no internal sense of myself, so that I can become someone only by showing that I am the smartest, quickest, most powerful, etc. Since my goal is to get as much money (or power) as possible, the measure of my validation is quantifiable and clear. I can then replace my empty void, where there should be self worth, with statistics (money, titles). By doing this, I can substitute the admiration of others for a sense of self worth.

If I don't accomplish these goals, I will:

...still have avoided having to make a examination of who I am. I will be of no value, since that is the message I have gotten, probably from childhood. I will have failed in life, since I believe that money and power are the purpose of our being here. My sense of security will be threatened, since I can't face life without a big pile of money in case "they" come after me.

There is nothing wrong with money or achievement. In parts of the Far East (ie: Japan) achievement can be the only goal. Thus, children commit suicide and adults die by the thousands of heart attacks because they didn't get into the right school or job. In the West, it is mostly money. Our literature is full of rags-to-riches hero stories. For these people there is nothing, or no one, that will stand in the way of their making "enough" money. For many, this is so indoctrinated in them from childhood that they will pursue this unquenchable quest until they die or it kills them.

In the Course, money and achievement don't exist as such. This is because that is not the purpose of the Course. There are many students of the Course who are extremely wealthy and/or poor. The Course's purpose is to give us another way to look at this world. The money-grubbing world we see is the result of our dreams of this world. The nightmare of this world is one we created when we created our separation from God.

The only sanity left in this world of insanity is the voice of the Holy Spirit. Once you believe that this is a world of insanity, it makes a lot more sense. There is no explaining the ways of this world. It is a world of money grubbing, social posturing, corruption, pain, misery, power seeking and, eventually, death. Running through all of this insanity, is a tiny voice inside of us; that of the Holy Spirit (HS). This is one of our most important gifts from God.

Whatever we do to climb out of this insane world we do with the help of HS, since we cannot do it alone. A fundamental belief of the Course is that all we have to do is to give HS a "little willingness." He will do the rest. HS asks only that we look at this world a little differently. This is what the Course calls the "real world." Basically, the real world is one where we admit this is a world of corruption, pain and death. But, we do not then conform to it, nor do we have to withdraw from the world in pursuit of "heaven."

In the real world, we look beyond money, title, education, shape, behavior or background to that loving holiness that exists in everyone. You may think that this is another unrealistic view of the world. You would, however, be well advised to hang in until we get to the punch line. The Course teaches that HS helps us to understand our dream of this world. In doing so, we begin to perceive that we not only made this world, but we also created our experiences in it.

Our Holy Spirit tells us that how we perceive this world is up to us. How we perceive it is how we will experience it. If we are invested in a PhD, money or power, that then, by definition, is our view of the world. If we can only see ourselves positively when we are a multi-degreed, rich person of power, what happens when we lose our job, our money, and the school of our degrees is closed in a scandal?

For most people, the symbols of this world are their identity, since they don't have any other. They have been told since childhood that they must be a professional or businessman and that they must make lots of money and live in "poshurbia" with their spouse and 2.5 children. Anything less and they are a "failure."

Following is exhibit 3f, which shows Course beliefs as opposed to worldly achievement beliefs.

MY COURSE BELIEFS AS AN ACHIEVEMENT STRIVER
exhibit 3f

Since I believe that I am not acceptable as I am, I can become acceptable by:

...believing that I am a holy, loving child of God. With this belief I can overcome my negative childhood programming. I can do this by training my mind about who I am.

I believe that I need to do this because:

...when I replace my drive for money and power with God I am like the recovered alcoholic who depends, for his recovery, on a higher power. I will then have the courage to face life's adversities without the emotionally devastating effect they have for someone with no self worth.

Or (fill in for you):

If I don't accomplish these goals, I will:

...have doomed myself to the frustrating life of never having enough. I will constantly worry about my financial condition, no matter how secure I may be financially.

Or (fill in for you):

A Course in Miracles in 5 Minutes

The choice then is whether you want to spend your life believing in this world or in your divinity. Below is exhibit 3g, which shows the difference. Notice how dramatic that difference is.

COMPARISON OF THIS WORLD BELIEF TO DIVINITY BELIEF exhibit 3g	
BELIEVING IN THIS WORLD RESULTS IN:	BELIEVING IN YOUR DIVINITY RESULTS IN:
• a great deal of stress • worrying about what might happen • complaining about what was • remembering your past guilt • the desire to "fix" other people • rehearsing what to say • analyzing what others say or do • collecting grievances • spreading worries • needing to place blame on others • venting or saving anger	Peace

A Course in Miracles in 5 Minutes

Chapter 4

Can I Actually Improve My Self Image?

Many thoughtful people have asked why people who have had difficulty changing their self image in other settings have been able to do so with the Course. It is because the Course starts and ends the journey to a new self image at a place that is usually only one of many steps for most other belief systems: a belief in the joyful divinity of every person.

Why the Course works

The Course is not without its own problems. As a mind trip, there is little or no socialization in most groups. The tendency is for people to come, discuss and to leave. Many people miss this human touch which they are used to in church, social or therapy groups. The Course can be boring as well. There are certain basic principles which are repeated in hundreds of different ways, in both the text and workbook. As a result it can be extremely repetitive.

One of the best ways to illustrate other differences is to compare the Course to other major methods for changing self esteem. In other methods, there seem to be one or all of three elements, which the Course does not have: 1. a wise man or guru, 2. a condoning or approval of anger, flowing from a belief in an angry God, and 3. money, or fees paid to get the knowledge.

The Course has, by its own dictates, no hierarchy, leaders or central management office. Study groups are led by volunteers who donate their time. Other than a very few nationally known figures who have written widely on the Course, there are no gurus of prominence in the Course. A student of the Course, in many metropolitan areas, has a choice of a number of study groups. He picks the one, or more, that fit him best. Since there generally is no charge, he is free to attend as many as he wants.

Compare this to most organized religions. They almost all: 1. have gurus, such as a priest, minister, rabbi, 2. believe in an angry God (ie: a God who is capable of anger about anything) and 3. have a need for money to support land, buildings, salaries, hierarchy, etc. The major difference is their support of an angry God. From this belief follows the ability to rationalize a split system of behavior (ie: God "smoted" all those people, so I can, too.).

Another comparison can be made to the numerous "12 step" groups such as Alcoholics...Co-Dependents...Incest Survivors...etc. Anonymous. All of these programs are first class, having helped millions of people. Steps two and three of AA's 12 steps are to give in to a higher power. That is essentially the only step in the Course. The only point of this comparison is that AA's belief that a person should go back over everything that has happened can be an invitation to get locked into endless negativity and anger. The Course looks at all seemingly negative past events as gifts. Further, the Course says that the perpetrator or antagonist is always ourself.

At first glance, a comparison to therapy or self help groups mostly involves money. There are innumerable therapists and positive thinking groups. Many are quite effective, some are not effective, and still others may be damaging. They have in common that they charge fees for their services and tend to create (many times reluctantly) gurus. The major difference between them and the Course is that they tend not to be spiritually based. If they are (ie: a "Christian" therapist) they believe in an angry God. This gives permission, indeed encouragement, to their patients to be angry. That anger can be destructive.

Anger as your indicator

Many have called low self esteem the curse of this planet. It probably is. If you improve your self esteem, your life will improve as well. This chapter is about how the Course can be used to improve your self esteem. A basic premise about your life is that when you improve your self esteem, your life will improve.

You may get a clearer understanding of this process by applying it directly to the four events in your life that make you most angry and the reason(s) why. You should not go forward in this book before completing exhibit 4a. If you truly cannot complete exhibit 4a, take a look at only the next exhibit, 4b.

FOUR MAJOR EVENTS CAUSING MY ANGER
AND THE REASONS WHY
exhibit 4a
This exhibit calls for your narrative description only.

Event 1	Reason why for event 1
Event 2	Reason why for event 2
Event 3	Reason why for event 3
Event 4	Reason why for event 4

A Course in Miracles in 5 Minutes

It usually is a lot easier to know what makes you angry than it is to know why they have this anger control over you. If you want to know about what makes someone "tick", find out what makes him angry. If you want to know who he is, as a person, find out why. For example, following is exhibit 4b, with the same four major events from exhibit 4a. To illustrate, I show them for myself and my own life.

FOUR MAJOR EVENTS CAUSING MY ANGER
AND THE REASONS WHY
exhibit 4b

Event 1 *When defenseless people are hurt.*	Reason why for event 1 *As a child I was basically abandoned in boarding schools without money or parents. As such, I experienced first hand the severe sexual molestation, physical and emotional beatings that are possible in such a defenseless situation.*
Event 2 *Corruption in public office.*	Reason why for event 2 *When I sought protection from the school administration, it only brought deeper and more severe problems, since the administration itself engaged in the same kind of behavior. Thus, the only result of complaints was beatings, rape and molestation.*
Event 3 *Unkindness, in any form, to children.*	Reason why for event 3 *For the same reasons shown in 1 and 2 above.*
Event 4 *Bigotry or prejudice toward anyone.*	Reason why for event 4 *As a child, one of the major reasons for my plight was that my father was Jewish and that I was in "Christian" schools. The clergy would actively preach that since the Jews killed Christ, they should suffer, and I did.*

A Course in Miracles in 5 Minutes

Perhaps exhibit 4b will help you to complete exhibit 4a. Do you see how clearly my major angers of today are caused by the events of my childhood? To measure the level of my anger about any one of these events, my remedy for all of them was the same: immediate public execution of the guilty person. That is a high level of anger, or stated in the reverse, a very low level of self esteem.

We make our own world

This raises one of the principles of the Course that can be most difficult for many people. It flows out of the Course belief that we bring our worst fears on ourselves. As the Bible says: "that which I feared came upon me." While you may not have a problem with this, how do you apply this to a child or other defenseless person? This is good to use as an illustration because it is a most extreme example of belief system causing a result.

To illustrate, there is an insanity defense raised by many child molesters: "The child seduced me". Of course, such a defense is crazy. However, in the teachings of the Course, something akin to that does happen. The molester, or perpetrator, will do his thing to or with some child because he is crazy and compulsive. The only question is, which child? He will tend to stay away from the high self esteem child and pick the one with a wounded or weak self esteem. That child seeking approval, solace or a friend then becomes the target because of that child's very insecurities. As a result, the child's already fragile ego is further and even more deeply damaged.

The Course says that nothing of this world can touch us if we believe that we are not separated from God. Of course, the reverse is true as well. Everything of this world will affect us if we believe that we are separated. All of our worst fears come from a belief in separation. Therefore, to the extent that we feel separated, we guarantee a terrible life.

We then expect, and we get, the worst that everyone has to offer. We prove that "there is some good in the worst of us and some bad in the best of us." We will, as separated people, always experience the bad, even in the best of us. We call that forth by our belief. This is the basis of a cornerstone of the Course. When we see ourselves as negative, we invite the negativity of others. A negative self image can be corrected by our belief that we are a holy, loving child of God. The purpose of the Course is to arrive at that joyous belief.

Perhaps seeing exhibit 4c, how this same exhibit might be completed by someone with that HLCG belief, would help.

FOUR MAJOR EVENTS CAUSING MY ANGER
AND THE REASONS WHY
exhibit 4c

Event 1 *When defenseless people are hurt.*	Reason why for event 1 *My belief, from the Course, is that no one is truly defenseless. I look at both the attacked and attacker's "call for love." The attacker, no matter how brutal, is seeking to avenge or to get attention. The answer to which may be his execution, but not for revenge.*
Event 2 *Corruption in public office.*	Reason why for event 2 *The reasons people seek public office in this world are seldom spiritual. As such, once in office they reflect their worldly motivation. That motivation reflects the insanity of this world. Forget it; I need to get on with my own life. The best way to address this insanity is to fix my own head.*
Event 3 *Unkindness, in any form, to children.*	Reason why for event 3 *The craziness of this world is reflected vividly in how people treat children. If an adult is crazy, he will seek a target for that insanity who cannot fight back. The ideal target can be a child. People do not tend to have children for spiritual reasons.*
Event 4 *Bigotry or prejudice toward anyone.*	Reason why for event 4 *Bigotry is one of the clearest signs of low self esteem. The bigot is, in Course terms, talking about himself. If he spent a small fraction of his bigotry energy on his low self esteem and spiritual values he would be bringing joy rather than rage into his life.*

As you can see, the Course addresses each issue in terms of you and your joy. Again, you cannot believe that you are a HLCG and be angry. This HLCG belief in itself will bring you higher self esteem. If you change from lower to higher self esteem, it will positively affect your life. Examples of this are the expectant businessperson, the confident job seeker, the popular student, the joyful child, the benevolent judge or the friendly clerk. The Course leads to a higher self esteem by working on each person's greatest spiritual void: their belief in separation from God.

The course principle is that you, not God, created this separation. When you feel separated from God you are also separated from your ability to be whole, loving, self accepting or accepting of others. Therefore, you can end your separation. When you end or narrow it, you are closer to being a holy, loving child of God. As a HLCG you will have, be and live joy. That is it!

Chapter 5

Applying Course Principles
to Your Relationships With People

In Course terms, we have two choices, the first of which is atonement. The second is separation. Separation results in living in the ego. The ego's primary weapon is anger. Anger is caused by fear. The underlying fear is of separation from and, thus, anger from God. This fear causes us to lash out at everyone, including ourselves. Anger, revenge, suspicion, envy, fighting, etc. is the result, and none of these makes life worth living.

Following is exhibit 5a, which will help you to clarify the way in which you relate to people. Again, there are no right or wrong answers. You will get the most benefit from this exhibit if you complete it without looking ahead.

HOW MY RELATIONSHIPS EVOLVE
exhibit 5a

I fill my needs for love and relationships by:

I keep these relationships by these techniques:

I pick my relationships on the basis of:

Because of these steps my relationships are:

As you review your responses, look for the pain versus joy in them. Many people experience their greatest pain in their relationships with others. The way in which they relate is a complicated series of "crutches" which they have built to enable them to stand up. They need these crutches because of their relationship-crippling beliefs.

The pain of relating for many people is severe. They tend, therefore, to answer the same questions put forth in exhibit 5a as shown in exhibit 5b.

HOW MY RELATIONSHIPS EVOLVE
exhibit 5b

I fill my needs for love and relationships by:

...trying to relate to people but, at the same time, by being constantly on guard to detect any problems in their actions. I am not quite sure what to look for. Mostly I am so starved for love and affection that I will overlook almost anything if people will just be nice to me. It always surprises me when they "turn on me" and I see the way they really are. Why didn't I see that before?

I keep these relationships by these techniques:

...hiding my anger, and sometimes rage, which I need to keep under control. It seems to me that most relationships are phony anyway. Much of it is meaningless conversation and insincere compliments, or just bitching and moaning about life. So, I just play along. However, I am almost always nervous when I am in a social situation. So, I cover it with bravado.

I pick my relationships on the basis of:

...trying to restrict myself to three kinds of people. First are those whom I can dominate, because they are even more dependent than I am. Second are those who are my traditional antagonists (the same kinds of people I have had trouble with before). But, this time I'm going to get it right or prove that I am now OK. Third is the person who wants something. I know it, but I go ahead with the relationship anyway.

Because of these steps my relationships are:

...mostly terrible. I keep turning over people in my life. I have little basis for any relationship. Since I don't know who I am, I can hardly know who they are. As soon as the confrontation starts I either accelerate it by strongly defending myself or I run from the relationship. I do this because personal attack is so difficult for me.

As you can see, this person is in real pain. Relationships for him tend to be like the moth to the candle. He gets burned every time. Applying the principles of the Course ends all of this. You will recall that we started this chapter by outlining two choices. The person above has picked the first one, separation.

The other choice is of atonement. In this we are a holy, loving child of God. As such we do not believe we are separated from God. We believe that He/She is on our side supporting us. We tend to see the godlike part of people and events, and therefore, tend to be joyous. A result is reasonably happy relationships. People who have joy and good self esteem tend to draw others with those same attributes to them.

The fear, planted by the ego, is that when we have this "unrealistic" belief in God, someone will take advantage of us. In fact, the reverse happens. It is those who are in their egos who find difficult people in their lives. They invite them in. A HLCG tends to exclude such people. This happens because he has only one goal - the joy and peace of the Holy Spirit. *Problem people don't tend to hang around peaceful "kooks" very long.*

How does one reach this utopia? The answer is the same as how to get to the concert stage or to the Super Bowl–practice. In the Course, we are practicing with our minds but our skills are developed with people instead of with a violin or a football. The Course makes two promises: 1. that all we need is "a little willingness" and 2. that every person is a gift to us, especially those we find the most difficult.

Our most difficult people are usually those we see regularly or someone who has played a significant role in our life. They may be our mother, father, child, sister, brother, aunt, uncle, boss, co-worker, or employee. When confronted with one of these people in their most difficult mode, the Course tells us exactly what to do. First, remember that you are a HLCG. Second, determine what part of the problem behavior comes from them and what part is from you. At some level, we tend to know when we are being an SOB instead of a HLCG. So far, this is not much different from the old adages of counting to 10 and knowing yourself.

How the Course differs from other belief systems

At this point, the Course departs dramatically from other belief systems. The points that are different about the Course are:

1. The "worse" people are, the more of a gift they are to you. This gift happens since the strength of your reaction shows how significant their behavior is to you.

2. When negative or hurtful people cause you pain, they are merely a mirror of your own belief system. If they were not a mirror, their behavior wouldn't bother you.

3. People can only do one of two things: give love or call for love.

4. A call for love can be as strong as an assault on you. The Course says to give love, most particularly when they are calling for it.

5. You don't need to worry about protecting yourself when you respond with love to the most negative calls for love. As a HLCG, you will be protected.

6. Your consistent barometer of whether you are responding with love is your intent. With a loving intent, you do what is necessary and it will be right.

7. One particular Course lesson is always applicable: "*if I defend myself, I am attacked.*" A HLCG has nothing to defend.

To more clearly see the difference between Course belief systems and other belief systems, compare the answers to the four questions in exhibit 5b with those in exhibit 5c on the opposite page. Then compare these two exhibits with your own answers in exhibit 5a.

HOW MY RELATIONSHIPS EVOLVE - COURSE VIEW
exhibit 5c

I fill my needs for love and relationships by:

...accepting all people as they come into my life. I know that I can respond to the best parts of them. If that part is so small that I cannot relate to them, I can lovingly end the relationship without causing them pain. My pain will be only that I could not help them in their path toward God. If they reject me because of who I am, they have given me a great gift, by enabling me to get on with my life without them.

I keep these relationships by these techniques:

...I am always loving and honest with people, both about who I am and who I perceive they are. When faced with any anger from them, I need only ask myself what this anger is for. I know it is a gift, and since I know that they are but a mirror of my own feelings, I look inside myself for the cause of that anger. This is not a matter of my being either right or wrong. I simply know that if there is hostility, I created it.

I pick my relationships on the basis of:

...the belief that from perception flows my reality. If I believe myself to be a HLCG, then no relationship can harm that part of me. In most relationships there is no need to share these beliefs with people. I can just go my way in peace and permit them to do the same.

Because of these steps my relationships are:

...a joy! I used to have a need to be constantly on guard and judgmental about each new person and action. Now, I can truly be with that person and hear all that he has to say. In this way, I grow from each encounter. I also have vast amounts of new energy available. This energy has been made available because I no longer need it to protect myself in my relationships. I use that energy to further my understanding of relationship building.

A Course in Miracles in 5 Minutes

Applying these Course principles can start a whole new cycle in our lives. The process of being in conflict with others can begin to have a life of its own. Remembering all of our prior hurts and problems takes a lot of time and energy. It also can become a habit pattern. *When one operates by collecting hurts, one automatically excludes most positive people from his life.* When one looks for the hurting behavior, as the Course promises, it is there. One also develops a long and detailed mental list of things that others can do to cause them pain. This pattern can go on endlessly.

Cataloging someone's "sins" against you with plans for revenge is all too common. There is a vast difference between this and what the Course suggests. To illustrate, contrast the cataloging of sins to simply remembering that this or that person may be someone with whom you may well have difficulty in building a close relationship. As the Course says, the difficult behavior that causes you to believe this, is in itself a gift. It forces you to examine if your own belief system is solid and loving.

The absence of "Sin"

The belief pattern that the Course suggests has two built-in self perpetuating benefits. The first is that there is nothing and/or no "sins" against you to catalog, let alone to be hurt about. Second, that when you are positive in your own beliefs, the aspect of people that you experience will change.

We only tend to have time for a small group of close relationships in any event. Therefore, another gift from positive beliefs is the automatic screening of who will participate in our life. As a result, we pre-select those people who will reinforce our loving belief system. We will also stop trying to develop "a wide circle of close friends" (a virtual impossibility). Many times the "wide circle of close friends" is an attempt to gain that acceptance which a person cannot give to himself.

Clearly, it is very difficult to go from one extreme in belief system to the other quickly. We need to remember that the path is marked by: 1) a little willingness, 2) reading and applying the lessons from the Course and 3) practice- practice- practice. As with any winning system, team, or belief, the goal is more than worth the effort.

Measuring your belief in "Sin"

For your convenience there is, in exhibit 5d following, a checklist that you can use to help you achieve the joy of discontinuing your "catalogs of sins." A handy measure of your progress, use the space provided in exhibit 5d for a numerical evaluation of your reactions after each encounter. Use the same evaluation system as in all other non-narrative exhibits. Number the strength of your agreement from 0 (neutral) to +10 (strong agreement) and from 0 (neutral) to -10 (strong disagreement). Questions about using this -10 to 0 to +10 ranking system are answered at the start of Chapter 1. This will give you a good measure of your reactions. Most of us have a good idea as to the depth of our feelings. Just assign a number to that intensity or depth of feeling. Then total and average the "score." For example, you may start out being an average "7" in Column B, Belief in Sinners, versus an average "3" in Column A, Belief in HLCG.

You do not have to use every line every time. You do have to use both columns A and B for any line you use. This gives balance and greater statistical accuracy to your average. Before you mark exhibit 5d, make copies to keep in your purse or wallet. As promptly as possible after each meaningful encounter, complete one to help evaluate you how you reacted. Keep your completed "5ds." Use them to measure changes in your belief system. Exhibit 5d may be copied.

CHECKLIST OF BELIEFS IN RELATIONSHIP JOY VERSUS "SINS"
exhibit 5d
(you do not have to answer all questions each time you use this)

Use a scale from -10 (strongly disagree) to 0 (neutral) to +10 (strongly agree). Your evaluation of your feelings can be anywhere on this scale. There is no "right" answer. Use the comments section at the bottom to write the ideas, based on your review of the results, about how to improve.

Date:_____Encounter with:_____at:_____

This encounter was about:_____

A. Belief in a HLCG		B. Belief in "sinners"	
Rank	Action or belief	Rank	Action or belief
	I saw his actions as love or a call for love.		I saw his actions as a personal attack. (1)
	I responded with love, no matter what his behavior.		I let him have "it", so he knows what a jerk he is. (2)
	I noted whether a close relationship is possible.		I made a mental catalog of his "sins" against me. (3)
	I looked for the gift. I know it is always there.		My anger at his outrageous behavior is justified. (4)
	As a gift, I can see the positive side of this.		I need to get away from it no matter what the cost. (5)
	They cannot hurt a HLCG; I let them be themselves.		I stayed in control so I would not get hurt. (6)
	I have no judgments about him or them.		I have carefully evaluated what they probably want. (7)
	TOTAL: add total of this column		TOTAL: add total of this column
	AVERAGE: divide total by number of spaces used		AVERAGE: divide total by number of spaces used

Comments:

You may feel that completing this exhibit was a lot of work. However, I would suggest that it is far less work than the continuing "festering" that we all tend to do when we have a negative encounter. Don't you always think of the things that you could have said? Depending on the severity of the encounter and its emotional importance, we may "turn it over in our minds" 10, 20, or more times.

Measuring your "little willingness"

Review how you turn things over in your mind and compare this to the criteria in column B of the last exhibit (5d). You will probably find that all of your "churning" about the encounter is from column B. Then take that past encounter and carefully review it for your possible reactions from column A. As you do this review, ask yourself if, during that particular encounter, you used any part of the HLCG belief system? Is it expressed in any of the seven questions in column A? If so, mark that change, no matter how small, in red, or some other clearly visible contrasting color.

You have just experienced what the Course calls "a little willingness." You are therefore on your path to joy in your life. Do this for the most recent encounter(s) that are troubling you and are vivid in your memory. Now that you have expressed a little willingness, use your copies. Whenever possible, after an encounter–stop and complete the form. You do not have to complete the comment sections at the same time. They can be for later reflection. It is, however, important to use the form promptly after each encounter.

Evaluating your answers to the seven "sin" questions

It may help to look at the balance between these seven questions. Each is numbered in the far right. Refer to those numbers in using this analysis. Question #1 "I saw his actions as . . . " is a threshold issue for the Course. It has often been said that the entire Course is in each of the Course's 365 lessons. Question #1 is a demonstration of that.

If you can get to the point where you can always see another's behavior as either love or a call for love, you will be practicing the Course. It may be easier to know when you are the recipient of love. A call for love can be difficult to identify as well as a difficult idea. It is the reverse of most of what we have been taught in this world. In its briefest form, the most direct attack on you can be the loudest call for love. The goal in the Course is to see such an attack as a call for love, and to respond with love.

This means not to return the attack. This is not a suggestion that you "turn the other cheek" or any other surface for the next attack. However you respond to an attack, the measure of the love in your response is in your intent. That is why question #2, "I responded with love" is next. In answering questions #1 and #2, it is important to remember that the Course does not have unrealistic expectancies. In the Course belief, it is unrealistic in this world to "turn the other cheek" and invite more of the same treatment. In this insane world, doing so would just be encouraging that insanity. However, in your attempt to avoid that insanity, the Course has no expectancy that you will immediately change all of your beliefs. Do not expect that you will make a marathon run and go from a -10 to a +10 on the scale. If, at the outset, you post some number better than where you have been, that is enough.

Question #3 addresses one of our most common traits in this world. We catalog, regurgitate, dwell on and endlessly recite another's "sins" against us. One of the most commonly asked questions is "and then do you know what he/she did?" All question #3 suggests is to note if this person can be other than a "special" relationship for you. A "special" relationship, in Course terms, is one that has other than a spiritual basis. It is a relationship in which one, or both, people are seeking something of this world from the other.

Question #4, "looking for the gift" is another idea which is the reverse of what we are taught in this world. Looking for the gift is one of the key bridges between a little willingness and a change to a positive attitude. After some practice you will begin to look for the gift in most events you see around you. You will begin to do this even if you are not personally involved. For example, news as presented by the media is usually given in its most negative form. Many studies have convinced the media that negativity is what most people want to hear. You will, however, begin to see positive aspects of even the most negative news.

Once you start seeing the gift, question #5 reflects a new way of life. You no longer need to flee the scene of negative events. You can now start to see a more balanced view of the people involved. Real people now start to populate your life. They replace the saints and sinners you are used to creating. In Course terms, the combination of being in your ego (low self esteem) and seeing people as "sinners" always results in your being a victim. As a victim, you bring out and experience the worst that people have to offer. You have self-fulfilling nightmares. When you change your self image, you will less frequently need to flee the scene of negative encounters. Knowing that they are a gift, you need only decide what that gift is and to act on it.

Question #6 measures how much you see yourself as a HLCG. When you do, you don't have to control the situation. You just let it be. A truism from the Course is that if you do not change to this HLCG view; your encounters and your life will just get worse. The Course tells us that if we do not change, each succeeding encounter (lesson) will become worse, to help us get the message.

Finally, question #7 measures your ability to be non-judgmental. This is an important goal of the Course. Imagine yourself walking into a car dealership, lawyer's or doctor's office, or a real estate or stock broker's office. These are all important decisions in this world. If you feel that these are the kind of people who are difficult and/or imperious and/or will try to stick you with a lemon and/or big fees for incompetent work, you will automatically select that kind of person. The difference, in the Course, is to recognize that this is a world of such problems. However, you do not have to accept that these are your problems. They do not need to exist in the life of a holy, loving child of God.

Why your mind changes your world

Therefore, your answers to exhibit 5d should reflect: (1) a knowing that this kind of negative rip-off work attitude may well be an all too common part of this world, but that (2) you, a HLCG, do not have to be a part of this world and therefore (3) do not have to be a victim of that insanity. As the Course says, you may be in this world, but you do not need to be of it. You recognize it exists. You simply see both others and yourself as above that. Your belief has the power to cause each to be a HLCG for you. Note that at the same time they might be a crook, or crazy, or incompetent to and for everybody else. If, however, your feeling is that you cannot bring this person around, even given your beliefs, you will go elsewhere since you will have the self esteem to do so.

Using this illustration, you will have applied the Course principles to an encounter. You no longer need to feel like a victim, because you won't be one. You have given up fear. That fear flowed from your belief in your separation from God. A purpose of this exercise is to change your belief in separation. When you feel that you are separated from an all powerful "enemy" (God) you will do yourself in before He can do it to you. Think of the rabbit who dies a thousand deaths as you approach him with love. His fear controls his life.

You will also be replacing life's struggle with a joy of life. As your view has changed, so have your actions. You no longer create a series of negative stories to prove how crooked and insane people can be. You no longer need to prove it; you know it is an inherent part of this world. What you are now trying to prove is that you have the power, as a HLCG, to overcome this world. With this as your goal, your life's story will change.

There are three steps in reaching this goal. These are, in order: (1) that you can change your actions by changing your beliefs, (2) that you can change your beliefs by using these Course ideas, and (3) that you have the power to change the actions of other people by changing your beliefs. Your use of exhibit 5e, following, may help you to have more confidence in these three steps. As with prior exhibits, your best benefit is to complete this exhibit without looking ahead in this book.

Measuring progress using Course principles to change your mind

Exhibit 5e is a full page, as are most exhibits. It has been specially designed for you to copy and take with you, because it will take a lot of thought to answer. You can use your alone, quiet, reflective time to do this. The three examples, designated "a" in each of the three sections, are the positive illustrations. These are the ways in which the Course has helped you to accomplish the goal. The three examples designated "b" are the ways in which the Course has not helped. There is no right or wrong answer.

CHANGES IN YOUR LIFE FROM CHANGES IN YOUR BELIEFS
exhibit 5e

This exhibit should be answered in narrative form, and will take some thought.

A. EXAMPLES OF THE EFFECT ON MY ACTIONS OF CHANGES IN MY BELIEFS
a. Three examples of belief changes that have changed my actions
1._____
2._____
3._____
b. Three examples of belief changes that have not changed my actions.
1._____
2._____
3._____

B. EXAMPLES OF CHANGING MY BELIEFS BY USING THESE IDEAS:
a. Three examples of belief changes from using Course ideas:
1._____
2._____
3._____
b. Three examples of non-belief changes from using Course ideas:
1._____
2._____
3._____

C. EXAMPLES OF CHANGING ACTIONS OF OTHERS BY CHANGING MY BELIEFS
a. Three examples of changing others' actions by my belief change
1._____
2._____
3._____
b. Three examples of not changing others' actions by my belief changes:
1._____
2._____
3._____

A Course in Miracles in 5 Minutes

Following is exhibit 5f which gives an example of how these questions can be answered. Use every effort to complete exhibit 5e before reviewing 5f. As is the case with most things in life, what you get out of this exercise will about equal what you put into it. This is particularly so when you are trying to rearrange your thinking and belief system. Trying your hardest to complete 5e before looking at 5f will be its own reward. This is so even if you don't complete 5e before looking ahead. The challenge of the thought required will help to reshape your thinking.

CHANGES IN YOUR LIFE FROM CHANGES IN YOUR BELIEFS
exhibit 5f

A. EXAMPLES OF THE EFFECT ON ACTIONS OF CHANGES IN MY BELIEFS
   a. Three examples of belief changes that have changed my actions
      1. When I began to believe that my older brother would help me, I was a lot more friendly to him.
      2. When I no longer believed that Santa gave presents to good girls, I didn't act worse at Christmas, I enjoyed it anyway.
      3. When I understood that if my production fell off on the job, I would be fired, I began looking for another job.
   b. Three examples of non-belief changes, so that I have not changed my actions.
      1. When I began to believe that my brother would help me, I was so angry that he hadn't helped me before that I did nothing.
      2. As a child, I sort of knew that Santa was not real anyway, so nothing really changed in how I got what I wanted.
      3. When I understood that if my production fell off on the job, I knew it was just another example of this lousy world.

B. EXAMPLES OF CHANGING MY BELIEFS BY USING COURSE IDEAS:
   a. Three examples of belief changes from using Course ideas:
      1. When my brother started to help me, I saw that he was a HLCG.
      2. Santa Claus is a reflection of my own beliefs. As a HLCG, I will by my love bring into my life what I practice.
      3. My job production requirement is a gift because I know that I must use Course principles to achieve it, or I will fail.
   b. Three examples of non-belief changes from using these ideas:
      1. When my brother started to help me, I knew he wanted something, because if there is anyone of this world it is him
      2. Now, as a woman, I know "Santa" is a man who is able to support me. Being a HLCG is one thing, but I need money.
      3. I may be employed by God, but I don't ever see his payroll check.

C. EXAMPLES OF CHANGING ACTIONS OF OTHERS BY CHANGING MY BELIEFS
   a. Three examples of changing others' actions by my belief change:
      1. When my brother started to help me, I saw him as a HLCG and, as a result, we are now close friends as well as brothers.
      2. Now, as a grown woman, I know that no man can be my "Santa." My spiritual life with a man will bring me what I need.
      3. I now can be straight with others. I do this by telling them my agenda. Their response is always more than I could want.
   b. Three examples of not changing others' actions by my belief changes:
      1. I know my older brother. Possibly some people can be a HLCG; he will never be. In spite of his help to me, he proved that by hitting me up for money right away.
      2. Men just are not capable of a spiritual relationship. They only want one thing. So I swap that for security.
      3. My spiritual life and my job are two different things.

A Course in Miracles in 5 Minutes

The questions and answers in exhibit 5f are meant to cover three important areas of our life in this world. These are, in the same order as the numbered questions: 1) social, 2) dependency, and 3) money. The sequence, as you may recall, for each of these three areas is also threefold. The three-step sequence is: 1) Can we change our actions based on changes in our beliefs? 2) Can we change our beliefs by using Course ideas? and 3) Can we change the actions of others by changing our beliefs?

Escaping a world of bigotry

Man as we, not God, have constructed him, is a "social animal." As a result, we tend to get entangled in all kinds of social problems. Because we do not believe ourselves and others to be holy, loving children of God, our feelings are easily hurt. This results in our: a) rejecting before we can be rejected, b) forming groups, cliques, religions, etc. where we can be with "our own" and 3) generally behaving in a socially bigoted way.

We have developed this social bigotry to such a high level that we have even institutionalized it. Thus, the structure of governments, businesses and religions all are designed to achieve this goal. We exclude women, minorities and countless others. Catholics exclude Protestants, both exclude Jews and vice-versa. There exists in the United States and many other of the "democracies" of the world, innumerable private clubs, the purpose for which is exclusion and bigotry. There is not a significant western religious sect or belief, with the possible exception of Bahai and Quaker, that does not engage in some form of organized exclusion or bigotry.

In our personal lives we have rampant divorce, employment firings or resignations and shifting personal loyalties. Entire industries have been built up around these socially destructive inclinations. In the United States some of those industries have more gross income than the entire income of some countries. Examples of this are family law (divorce) attorneys, therapy, executive and administrative recruiting.

To all of this the Course simply says that when you love yourself as a HLCG, you will love your brother. Then you will not tend to experience this turmoil. Each of the "#1" questions in exhibits 5e and 5f is designed to illustrate this HLCG change in a social setting.

Using the belief
Life changing questions

There are six questions which show the social results of the Course. They are all numbered "1." They are: Aa1, Ab1, Ba1, Bb1, Ca1 and Cb1. Look at your answers to these questions in exhibit 5e and compare them, for intent, to the answers in exhibit 5f. To illustrate, use the answers in Aa1 and Ba1: "When I began to believe that my brother...". Notice the difference between being angry at what was past and gone (Ab2) and simply responding positively to the brother's help (Aa1). In Course terms the past is meaningless. It does not exist. Therefore, to save up past hurts is to void the possibility of getting much joy from the Course.

Focus on the answer in Aa1 and ask one question: why? The Course is built on intent. Being "a lot more friendly" in order to get something will not, in Course terms, work. An example of this would be getting more of whatever the material stuff of this world was that the brother was handing out. This would not be the Course. The friendliness should reflect seeing the brother as a HLCG. Look at the answers to Ba1 and Ba2. These clearly illustrate this spiritual difference in viewpoint.

There are no good deeds as such in the Course. The Course looks at intent and says that if you do an act only for public consumption, while intending something else, the only person you have fooled is yourself. To illustrate this, look at the answers to Ca1 and Ca2. The Course would say that when we see our brother as a HLCG, it doesn't make any difference if he wants money. We will deal with that issue on its Course merits as well.

A way in which we get to see others as HLCG is by realizing that we are not dependent on them. Dependency can, in Course terms, be simply a form of idolatry. Or worse, it can be a confirmation of our belief in separation from God. We are dependent on others when we believe that: 1) they can do for us that which we cannot do for ourselves or 2) they have some kind of power or ability we do not have or 3) they are somehow superior to us.

The answers numbered "2" are designed to illustrate this. Thus, "Santa would give me presents if I was a good girl" (Aa2) reflects her belief that her actions were not designed to get material results but rather to live in joy. Contrast this to question Ab2 "nothing really changed in how I got what I wanted." What she wanted was something other than joy. Notice how, in her answers to Ba2 and Ba3, she is developing these beliefs into her life's statement. Clearly, she is headed for joy in Ba2 and for trouble in Bb2.

She expresses the ultimate, and really only, result of these two divergent beliefs in Ca2 and Cb2. In Cb2 she has become essentially a prostitute, swapping sex for money. She does this by downgrading men as "non-spiritual" and as wanting only sex from women. In Ca2 she sees her ability to reach an even closer relationship with God by joining with the man in her life for that goal. That brings us to the final series of answers numbered Cb 1,2 and 3. They reflect our views about money and how we relate money to our spiritual beliefs. The most dramatic examples of this are shown in the difference between the answers to Ca3 and Cb3.

"Being open with others" (Ca3) in a business or professional context is a major meeting point of the Course and this world. This conflict can be such a basic part of our lives that it tends to be the point that many people cannot resolve. Therefore, it deserves separate treatment. The Course gives us the courage to be open. This courage flows from our belief in ourselves as a HLCG. The result is the same as for any behavior, positive or negative. It becomes self-reinforcing.

Chapter 6

How the Course Eliminates Fear
And Helps You to be Open

When you know who you are and you are comfortable about it, you are more open with people. You are most open when you believe both they and you are holy, loving children of God (HLCG). This openness can change your life, and enable you to experience new and better relationships in every aspect of your life. This chapter is about the benefits of being open and how this can be achieved with A Course in Miracles.

Being open means your willingness to face any challenge to you, your beliefs, your life or your goals. If you are open you have no secrets. Therefore, you face these challenges with peace, love, forgiveness and joy. That last one, joy, may be a problem. Why would you face a difficult challenge with joy? Because in the Course all such challenges are gifts. When you believe that your darkest secrets are gifts of joy, they are no longer secrets. The Course eliminates secrets by your belief that you are a HLCG. As such, you have no need to be closed.

Knowing your fears

The basic reasons why your life changes because of the Course are: 1. you will have few fears (As a result you will be perceived more positively.), 2. you will truly love your brother so that he is not a threat to you, and 3. you will accept this insane world as it is. Since you expect nothing more than insanity in this world, you are not disappointed. This does not mean that you need to be part of it.

The first step on your road to openness is for you to understand why you have fears about being open. Below is an exhibit 6a to help you outline your fears of being open and the benefit of being open. As is the case with all exhibits, do your best to complete it before looking ahead in this book. Use the same -10 to +10 scale as in previous exhibits. You can be in strong disagreement with a statement even though it reflects your own fears. For example, you can be behaving according to a given fear and disagree with that fear, but be unable to control your behavior.

FEARS VERSUS BENEFITS FROM BEING OPEN
exhibit 6a

After you have written your statements, rank them by the degree of your agreement with them. Use 0 to mean being basically neutral about the statement and -10 to +10 to indicate the strength of your disagreement or agreement.

A. My three main fears about being open are:	(+10 to -10)
1._____	_____
2._____	_____
3._____	_____

B. The three main benefits to me from being open are:	(+10 to -10)
1._____	_____
2._____	_____
3._____	_____

A Course in Miracles in 5 Minutes

Again, there are no right or wrong answers in these exhibits. The only answer that is important is the one that best expresses how you feel. Ranking the intensity of your feelings enables you to scc how strongly you feel about your three main fears and benefits. Almost all reasons for not being open with others are based on fears of one kind or another. Many people rationalize the behavior flowing from their fears. Examples of these rationalized fear-driven behaviors generally fall into two broad categories. The first group can be the fearful person who is either "a man of few words" or extremely talkative. His behavior can similarly be either highly demonstrative or withdrawn. Either extreme is usually caused by fear. The second example are those who are generally bored with people. The Course would say that both of these are only symptoms, and that the root cause of both can be fear.

The Course is a journey to God, marked by shedding much of one's "protective" clothing of this world along the path. The traveler discovers that he does not need to cloak his life in silence to protect secrets or to withdraw to protect ego. When people become holy, loving children of God, there are few secrets and little ego left.

It is not reactions, but underlying reasons for those reactions that the Course considers. Therefore, by understanding your underlying reasons, you can change your reactions, including your openness.

Comparing your fears to those of others

To illustrate this comparison, following are exhibits 6b and 6c. They are the same as exhibit 6a. They have now been completed twice. Exhibit 6b is answered in the way that many people who live in fear might answer these six questions. This is without the benefit of Course principles. Exhibit 6c is completed by applying Course principles. You should evaluate your reactions to the statements made in each of these two exhibits. Use the same scale of -10 to +10, with +10 being in strong agreement and -10 being totally opposed, to the statements shown.

FEAR VERSUS BENEFITS FROM BEING OPEN
exhibit 6b

After you have written your statements, rank them by the degree of your agreement with them. Use 0 to mean being basically neutral about the statement and -10 to +10 to indicate the strength of your disagreement or agreement.

A. My three main fears about being open are:	(+10 to -10)
1. People will laugh at me if they know how I really am.	_____
2. I will lose all of my friends.	_____
3. There are lots of things people should never share.	_____

B. The three main benefits to me from being open are:	(+10 to -10)
1. The realization that my life is not really working the way it is.	_____
2. If I could be open about myself I would be happier.	_____
3. Maybe people will accept me the way I really am.	_____

A Course in Miracles in 5 Minutes

The statements in Section A show the very problems that the Course addresses. First, in answer to A1, "People will laugh at me if they know how I really am." How are you, really? Is it your fears, perversions, fantasies or problems at which they will laugh? Why will they laugh?

The Course says that your concern about ridicule flows from three truths: 1. You would laugh at them if the circumstances were reversed, so you are projecting, 2. If you believed you were a HLCG, you would have no fear of discovery of anything, so you need to rethink who you believe you are, and 3. You will have more confidence in people when you see them as HLCG, so you need to rethink what you believe other people are. The Course responses to statements A2 and A3 are the same as those to A1.

The statements in Section B need more analysis. Statement B1, "The Realization that my life is really not working . . . " tends to be a common motivation for people who get into the Course. Most people whose lives are not working are closed. They may complain widely and loudly about the problems in their life, however, they don't say much about the beliefs that caused their problems.

Many of these people realize that if they could be more open (Statement B2) about the causes, their life would improve. Please note that this is not permission to complain. It is the opposite of complaining, since they would only be complaining about themselves. They wonder if they might be acceptable just as they are (Statement B3). The Course would say, in the words of the old hymn: "just as I am, take me Lord, just as I am."

Following is exhibit 6c. Note section B, redone as a Course student might complete it. As you can see, the tentative steps in this section change to more determined statements. It will be helpful for you to again rank your feelings about these statements. Use the scale of -10 to +10, with +10 being in strong agreement and -10 being totally opposed to the statement.

BENEFITS FROM BEING OPEN - COURSE VIEW
exhibit 6c

Benefits of openness in accordance with Course Beliefs. Use 0 to mean being basically neutral about the statement and -10 to +10 to indicate the strength of your disagreement or agreement.

B. The three main benefits to me from being open are:	(+10 to -10)
1. My openness acknowledges everyone as a HLCG.	_____
2. As a HLCG I have nothing to fear from openness.	_____
3. My own spiritual growth requires that I act openly.	_____

A Course in Miracles in 5 Minutes

Note that the theme in both questions, B1 and B2, is the recognition of the person as a holy, loving child of God. This recognition requires only that you first see yourself as a HLCG. You will then be able to see the other person as a HLCG as well. Statement B3, "My own spiritual growth requires that I act openly", is an example of what the Course calls "a little willingness."

A little willingness starts us on the self perpetuating upward spiral toward joy. The negativity that surrounds most people leads them into a negative downward spiral. Being closed, suspicious, hateful and angry becomes its own self-fulfilling prophesy, and is how people get their lives into trouble to begin with. The opposite of that is how the Course lifts us out of trouble.

Your numerical rankings will show you the depth of your feelings about these statements. How strongly you feel will be determined by how deep your messages are. For example, it would take a longer time to sell the message of the Course to a member of a white supremacy group than to a member of the Salvation Army. Since the Course is a course in mind training, its goal is to change your existing belief system.

Understanding your basic beliefs

We are all controlled to some extent by our genetic programming. Many of our beliefs are, however, controlled by our childhood messages. To a large extent the purpose of the Course is overcoming the latter, largely negative, messages. We have all been raised on a diet of cautions and applause. Usually much more of the former than the latter. This results in many messages and memories operating all the time, trying to "protect" us from danger.

Whenever we feel that need for protection, we tend to get angry or defensive or we withdraw. Withdrawal, in our society, is common. The most common method of withdrawal is to be closed. We simply don't express how we feel. Use exhibit 6d to see where you are in this type of withdrawal behavior. First, for each topic, select the column (open or not open) that fits your beliefs, then jot down briefly your reason in that column.

If you have mixed feelings, use both columns and give your reasons in both. Then rank your feelings. Use from -10 (strongly disagree) to +10 (strongly agree). You can strongly disagree, for example, when you have a childhood message that controls you, but you don't like it. This is then a reflection of the beliefs that control you. Since the Course does mind training, it is helpful to know what your beliefs are before you set out on a mind training journey. For now, just complete the exhibit. We will talk about using the totals and averages later. As usual, do not look ahead since doing so may influence your answers.

WHAT SHOULD I BE OPEN ABOUT?
exhibit 6d

Items are listed alphabetically. Rank your feelings from -10 (strong disagreement) to +10 (strong agreement). This has to do with your feelings, so be open. Use the blank spaces for notes to yourself about the reason(s) for your feeling as you do. Add the total of each column and divide by 10, if you used all 10 items, or divide by the number used. You are ranking your feelings.

Item	A. Open Because	Rank	B. Not Open Because	Rank
1.GOD				
2.HATE				
3.HOPE				
4.LAW				
5.LEARNING				
6.LOVE				
7.MAN				
8.MORALITY				
9.THINKING				
10.TRUTH				
Add all numbers	TOTAL		TOTAL	
Divide by 10 (or # used)	AVERAGE		AVERAGE	

A Course in Miracles in 5 Minutes

If our life messages are accurate, lifelong protection is the result. If they are inaccurate, problems are the result; in some cases, quite severe problems. "Accurate" answers means that they reflect your truth about how the world and people really are. Our messages are usually accurate about the world (ie: "A stitch in time saves nine."). They are usually inaccurate about people (ie: "You have to be careful about bankers, blacks, Baptists, builders, bartenders, beauticians, botanists, etc."). The Course says that any such warnings about groups are not true. However, it also says that you can depend on almost every group in this world being caught up in such warnings, which are part of the insanity of this world.

Following is exhibit 6e, with various famous messages or "sayings." Rank your feelings about these in the space provided. Use a scale of -10 to +10, with +10 being in strong agreement and -10 being totally opposed to the statement. If you have no feelings one way or the other, use 0. There is no problem in partially believing conflicting statements. Thus, in the statements about God (#1) you can partially believe both "a" and "b." For example, you might rank statement 1a (Nietzsche) a +2 and statement 1b (Luther) a +8. You might also rank 1a as a -10 and 1b a +10, or the reverse of this. The point is there is no right or wrong answer, only a reflection of your beliefs.

MY RANKING OF MY BELIEFS ABOUT FAMOUS SAYINGS exhibit 6e	
Rank your feelings: -10 is opposed, +10 is agreement. Rank your feelings about both statements (a) and (b) in each numbered section, on the left.	
(+10 to -10)	1. about GOD a. "a thought that makes crooked all that is straight" - Nietzsche *or* b. "a mighty fortress" - Martin Luther
	2. about HATE a. "a tonic, it makes one live, it inspires vengeance" - Balzac *or* b. "the coward's revenge for being intimidated" - George Bernard Shaw
	3. about HOPE a. "the most treacherous of human fancies" - George Fenimore Cooper *or* b. "a waking dream" - Aristotle

	exhibit 6e *(continued)*
(+10 to -10)	4. about LAW a. "an ordinance of reason for the common good" - St. Thomas Aquinas *or* b. "a sort of hocus-pocus science" - Charles Macklin
	5. about LEARNING a. "the cobweb of the brain, Profane . . . and vain" - Samuel Butler *or* b. "a kind of natural food for the mind" - Cicero
	6. about LOVE a. "love is a malady without a cure" - John Dryden *or* b. "love is the true seed of every merit in you" - Dante
	7. about (humanity) MAN a. "a pliable animal...accustomed to everything" - Dostoevsky *or* b. "the most intelligent animal, and the most silly" - Diogenes
	8. about MORALITY a. "a private and costly luxury" - Henry Adams *or* b. "...how we may make ourselves worthy of happiness" - Immanuel Kant
	9. about THINKING a. "hardest work . . . the reason so few engage in it" - Henry Ford *or* b. "...to capture reality by means of ideas" - Jose Ortega y Gasset
	10. about TRUTH a. "truth is what most contradicts itself" - Durrell *or* b. "truth is what stands the test of experience" - Albert Einstein

A Course in Miracles in 5 Minutes

Your (childhood) messages and beliefs can be measured by reviewing your rankings in exhibit 6e. The Course is based on an absolute belief in God. Therefore, to the extent that you are wavering in your belief, you will have problems using the Course to change your life. Hate cannot coexist with Course beliefs. If you have some of Balzac (2a), rather than Shaw (2b), in your beliefs you can truly use the Course. George Bernard Shaw could not have better expressed A Course in Miracles when he called hate "a coward's revenge." The Course is clear about this. When we hate, the person we hate is really ourselves.

Hope may "spring eternal" in the human breast, but if you view hope as a fool's paradise, you will have problems with the Course. It is a Course in hope. Therefore, see how you ranked yourself on Cooper's (3a) view versus Aristotle (3b). As the Course evolves in your life, it will change to give real meaning to Aristotle's "waking dream."

The Course's view of the law of this world is that it is, like everything else in this world, insane. It is not order among men that the Course opposes. It is rather the worship of the meaning of most laws, many of which are conflicting and insane, and most of which do not work. The Course would say that this is an example of a group of people being trained to worship the insanity of this world (ie: many lawyers, overzealous prison guards, and politicians). The result is Course agreement with Macklin's (4b) "hocus-pocus science" rather than the "ordinance of reason" of Aquinas (4a).

Learning is a cornerstone of the Course, since it is about mind training. Therefore, if you tend to agree with Butler (6a) that learning is "the cobweb of the brain" rather than Cicero (6b) "a...natural food for the mind," you will find yourself resisting the Course. Feeling comfortable with Course principles requires most people to learn, or relearn, many basic principles of life. It takes lots of time, lectures, "book work" and thinking.

The Course is also a training to seek love. This does not mean the love of this world. The Course calls this "special love." Examples of special love are: I love you–if you make money, have sex, have sex in a certain way, fix me a good dinner, listen to my gripes, etc. These are examples of dependencies and addictions, not love. They are as Dryden (6a) says, "a malady without a cure." The love of the Course is a love of another holy, loving child of God. As such, that person can do no wrong. You can only love like this when you love yourself in the same way. Dante (6b) said it nicely: "Love is the true seed of every merit in you."

Our view of our fellow man is a result of our acceptance of the insanity surrounding us. The purpose of the Course is to bring us back to this reality. Dostoevsky (7a) summed it up by describing us as "a pliable, animal . . . accustomed to everything." That is the view of the Course as well. We therefore, as Diogenes (7b) said, have become "both the most intelligent and the most silly animal at the same time." As the centuries have progressed, large groups of humans strongly supported whatever the current madness of the planet may have been. The list is endless. However, a few examples are witch burning, human sacrifice, the Inquisition, the Crusades, the Holocaust, Japanese internment, ethnic cleansing, etc.

Morality and the Course are the same thing. The Course changes one's mind so that one can lead a more moral life. This is not however the morality so beloved of this world. That morality usually includes bigotry and leads to the insanity of this world. The morality of the Course is a much higher calling. It has no worldly ambitions or desires. It is moral because we see others as our brothers in Christ, regardless of how they see themselves. Kant (8b) is right. Behaving in this way makes us "worthy of happiness." Adams' view (8a) is the opposite of the Course. Morality is far from a luxury; we cannot reach God without the ladder of morality.

Statements 9 and 10 are tied together. This is a Course in mind training to conduct a search for truth. Both Ford (9a) and Gasset (9b) express this beautifully. It is hard work. The Course itself says that it is not for everyone. The Course goal is exactly as set forth by Jose Ortega y Gasset (9b): to "capture reality by means of ideas".

One person's reality may be another's poison, or as Durrell (10a) says, "truth is what most contradicts itself." However, this is not so in Course terms. The Course tells us that it does not have the only road to truth ("there are a thousand paths"), but that there is only one truth. All roads are equally good. That truth must, however, "stand the test of experience" as Einstein (10b) said.

Measuring change

Only you can answer this question for yourself: What works in your life? Once you find what works, the rest is relatively easy.

Exhibit 6f is the same exhibit you completed earlier as exhibit 6d. Try your hand at it again, using the principles you have just reviewed. If necessary, you can simply use the numbered statement identifications from exhibit 6e. However, do rank your feelings in any event. The goal is to see if your ranking totals and averages change, and in what way, as a result of putting your best effort into exhibit 6e.

Again, it is to your benefit not to look ahead. First complete each statement. Then rank your answers in the same way you did in the earlier exhibit. You probably will experience some change which may be significant. It is probably also temporary, since our minds, like rubber bands, tend to snap back to our original beliefs. The goal of the Course, to use this analogy, is to change the shape of the rubber band.

WHAT SHOULD I BE OPEN ABOUT?
exhibit 6f

Items are listed alphabetically, not in order of importance. Rank your feelings from -10 to +10. There is no right answer. This is about feelings. Use the blank spaces for any brief notes to yourself about the reason(s) for your feeling as you do. Add the total of each column and divide by 10, if you used all 10 items, or divide by the number used. You are ranking your feelings.

Item	A. Open Because	Rank	B. Not Open Because	Rank
1.GOD				
2.HATE				
3.HOPE				
4.LAW				
5.LEARNING				
6.LOVE				
7.MAN				
8.MORALITY				
9.THINKING				
10.TRUTH				
Add all numbers	TOTAL		TOTAL	
Divide by 10 (or # used)	AVERAGE		AVERAGE	

A Course in Miracles in 5 Minutes

Now compare your responses to the same questions in exhibits 6d and 6f. Look for differences. These are probably the areas in which you can make your most productive initial changes by using the Course. This is because these are the areas where you are most open to change. Pick the one or two which you would most like to change and make a commitment to yourself to do so.

There are three ways to measure your changes. These are by any differences in: 1) total scores, 2) average scores and 3) individual statements. Your total scores give you a sense of the changes, if any, in your balance between being open versus being closed. The average scores give you two good benchmarks. Thus, you can evaluate which individual statements are above and below your average. Your goal is to increase the rating of your lowest ranking "open" individual statements. You can pinpoint them and try to get them at least up to your average of all rankings. The reverse is true for the highest ranked "not open" statements. You want to lower these rankings.

Finally, your rankings of individual statements gives you a clear idea about your beliefs. The lowest rank "open" and highest ranked "closed" statements are probably where your most difficult work will be. In Course terms, they are also your greatest gift. If you view them as gifts, you will be able to deal with them much easier.

Another way to compare your results

It may be helpful for you to see how a strong Course student might answer the same questions. Exhibit 6g has been completed to show this.

WHAT SHOULD I BE OPEN ABOUT?
exhibit 6g

Items are listed alphabetically, not in order of importance. Rank your feelings from -10 to +10. There is no right answer. This is about feelings. Use the blank spaces for notes to yourself about the reason(s) for your feeling as you do. Add the total of each column and divide by 10, if you used all 10 items, or divide by the number used. You are ranking your feelings.

Item	A. Open Because	Rank	B. Not Open Because	Rank
1.GOD	*no fear as an HLCG*	+8	*fears close me down*	+2
2.HATE	*it takes away my peace*	+7	*watch out for "them"*	+3
3.HOPE	*my growth gives hope*	+6	*sometimes I wonder*	+3
4.LAW	*the only law is God's*	+9	*worldly law is power*	+5
5.LEARNING	*it's work, but it works*	+9	*rather be having fun*	+4
6.LOVE	*love frees me for joy*	+7	*I get scared*	+5
7.MAN	*my brother in Christ*	+8	*man is out to get me*	+4
8.MORALITY	*is not of this world*	+8	*money is wonderful*	+5
9.THINKING	*have to change my mind*	+9	*this is hard work*	+2
10.TRUTH	*there is only one*	+8	*the sly ones win*	+3
Add all numbers TOTAL		+79	TOTAL	+36
Divide by 10 (or # used) AVERAGE		+7.9	AVERAGE	+3.6

A Course in Miracles in 5 Minutes

Notice that even this strong Course student (me) has his doubts. Thus, while I have little fear as a holy, loving child of God (+8 in B1), I still can close down with fears (+2 in B2). I know that hate takes away my peace (+7 in A1), but my hate messages are hard to erase and so sometimes I worry about "them" (+3 in B2). My past growth has given me lots of hope (+6 in A3), but it can be such hard work that sometimes I wonder whether or not it is worth it (+3 in B3). I know that God's law is it (+9 in A4). However, I feel a big pull from the money and power flowing from the laws of this world (+5 in B4).

The mind training part of the Course is hard for everyone. It is like taking a Phd. I know learning is necessary (+9 in A5), but I would often rather be lazy and having fun (+4 in B5). Love, under all conditions, is a learned habit. I know that if I can always love, (+7 in A6) it gives me the ultimate joy. However, I worry that I will be taken advantage of (+5 in B6). This ties right in with how I view people. Notice that the answers are about the same as those to love, in 5 immediately above. Thus, I see man (or woman) as my brother/sister in Christ (+8 in A7), but continue to worry that he/she is out to get me (+4 in B7).

Our western culture has an obsession with money. It is here that our morality is most tested. I recognize that morality is of God and not of this world (+8 in A8), but still have a hard time getting out of my money fixation (+5 in B5). Notice the similarities in the answers to thinking (+9 in A9 and +2 in B9) to the answers to learning. In Course terms, it is harder to think than to learn. Thinking in the Course requires that you have learned the principles and that you are rearranging your thoughts to change your mind.

Finally is that ultimate quest of mankind–truth. You may believe, as I do, that there is only one truth, (+8 in 10A) but sometimes see the "crooks" winning (+3 in 10B). As a result, sometimes I vacillate. I console myself with the thought that there is lots more that I do not know or understand than that which I do.

Retake these quizzes as you progress in the Course. They can be a good measure of your growth.

Chapter 7

Practical Applications at Work

There is a basic theme about A Course in Miracles and your work. Your personal beliefs make far more difference in your work life than does either your type of job or your type of employer, because:

- The requirements of your type of job and of your employer are both elections which you have made, and therefore are determined by your personal beliefs.
- Money (the reason most people work) is a result, not a cause, of decisions made about type of job and employer.
- Interpersonal "skills" tend to mask the problem, which is you. As such, they tend to delay the solution.

In understanding this, we will debunk three commonly held ideas. These are:

- "If only I were able to be in X or Y job or industry, my life would be better."
- "There is nothing I can do about the amount of money I earn, because everybody is out to rip me off for their own personal gain."
- "If I know how to handle people, I can overcome these problems."

The journey to these Course beliefs requires us to address several issues before we arrive. The Course view is that we create our world by our beliefs. First we will take a detailed look at how that happens in the workplace. Then we will look at what to do about it in Course terms. The Course sums this up in lesson 22, as follows:

"What I see is a form of vengeance"
Today's idea accurately describes the way anyone who holds attack
thoughts in his mind must see the world. Having projected his anger on
the world, he sees vengeance about to strike at him. His own attack is thus
perceived as self defense. This becomes an increasingly vicious circle
until he is willing to change how he views the world. Otherwise, thoughts
of attack and counter-attack will preoccupy him and people his entire
world."   (from: A Course in Miracles)

Our workplace becomes a battleground where our ego fears are most able to take hold of us. The Course defines our ego as the opposite of our God self. The ego is our belief that we are a separate self. Our ego would say that since we are separate from everyone else, we are therefore separate from God. If we are separate, our gains need to be someone else's losses. Therefore we need, in the ego's view, to plot, attack, maneuver, outwit and win. We need to do this quickly–before someone else does it to us.

The Course says simply; love your brother as a holy, loving child of God, and the rest is easy. This is the clear contrast between the two belief systems.

Is the love principle applicable everywhere?

You may be thinking that the Course's approach to love may be great if you are a priest, minister or rabbi, but that it won't work in your business, industry, school, agency, department, plant, office, store, company, district, division, ship, platoon, prison, university, etc. Even if it could work here, it can't be applied in my job, management, sales, production, administrative, medical, legal, teaching or prison function. The type of product, service, function or purpose may be different in each one. But, there is one constant: you. That constant can be changed by changing your belief system.

To demonstrate that the ego belief system does not work anywhere, whereas love does, we can take a look at an extreme example: a front line military combat fighter who is drafted, and therefore not there by choice. Can you love your enemy across the sights of loaded weapon? The "enemy" in this extreme example, is the opposing soldier. The "enemy" in most of our lives is our boss, parent, employee, child, co-worker, salesman, spouse or competitor. Their behavior, in our view, may be outrageous. How we respond is the test.

If your intent is to kill your brother, you need to be wily, quick, smart, deadly and clever. This, however, reflects the separateness of the ego. If your intent is to be compassionate, and to see your brother as a HLCG, you need to want your brother (even when he is an opposing soldier) to live. That he may not want the same for you is irrelevant. Does this sound like setting yourself up for failure or death?

If you see the enemy in your gun sight as an evil adversary who is committing sin against you and the world, you clearly should shoot to kill and quickly. This is the basis of the continuous "holy wars" of the Middle East. If you see him as a HLCG you may still have to pull the trigger, but with a totally different intent. Your intent is not to kill a "sinner" or enemy, but to respond to his call for love in the only way possible. At this point, this may sound absurd. By the time you finish this chapter it may not seem so strange.

Belief changes versus interpersonal skills

This is not about the effects (results) of your belief system. Effects are your behavioral styles or interpersonal skills. It is about the root cause of those effects: your beliefs. There is a great tendency in our society to become expert in the "lingo" of interpersonal behavior. The idea is that then you can identify the other person's behavior. Hundreds of seminars have charged millions of dollars for this information. Once behaviors are identified, you can use one of a number of "formula" approaches to most effectively sell, convince, negotiate or manipulate. These formulas can work, but they take a lot of energy and don't address the problem.

The problem most often is your beliefs. The Course says "from my perception flows my reality." In this way, the Course changes you, rather than building an elaborate defense system supporting your insanity. These defense systems include many of the popular interpersonal skills and people-handling courses or "trainings". These trainings offer you the ability to cope, for awhile, with your own strange behavior. However, they tend to have two problems.

The first problem is that you will need to keep coming back for more training since you are still the same old SOB you always were. The only real difference is that you are now an SOB with some new manipulation skills. The second problem is that, as a result you become a wolf in sheep's clothing, (an SOB with manipulation skills) and so you create big-time internal conflicts for yourself. These conflicts are a leading cause of health issues like heart failure, cancer and depression. As one leading cartoon character says, "We have met the enemy, and it is us."

Interpersonal skills courses do have value. However, that value is created after you have changed yourself. Then your understanding of the reasons why people, including you, behave in insane ways can help you in meeting their real needs. By using Course principles, you will be meeting their (and your) real needs. This happens because you will refuse to see them as less than a holy, loving child of God.

Following is exhibit 7a, illustrating the beliefs of a typical interpersonal skills training.

PERSONALITY CHARACTERISTICS
IN A TYPICAL "PEOPLE SKILL" TRAINING
exhibit 7a

HIGH RESPONSIVENESS (+10)

AMIABLE STYLE Likes group interaction, but is not a good results-getting leader *solution:* project an interest in him	**EXPRESSIVE STYLE** Likes involvement, but can't stay focused *solution:* force yourself to go slowly, don't argue
ANALYTICAL STYLE Cautious, wants data and firm structure *solution:* be specific with high organization of topics	**DRIVER STYLE** Controlling, but low people empathy *solution:* don't get personally close and don't criticize

LOW ASSERTIVENESS (-10)   HIGH ASSERTIVENESS (+10)

LOW RESPONSIVENESS (-10)

A Course in Miracles in 5 Minutes

On the following page is exhibit 7.1b. It is similar to 7a. This is a sample exhibit, illustrating the way in which exhibit 7.2b should be completed. The sample exhibit shows "M" plots and "O" plots in each style area (amiable, expressive, etc.). "M" represents "Me", and "O" represents my "Opponent". A grid has been added to help position the points. Note the (-10) and (+10) shown on top, bottom and sides. The points were then connected, using a solid line for the "M" points, and a dotted line for the "O" points.

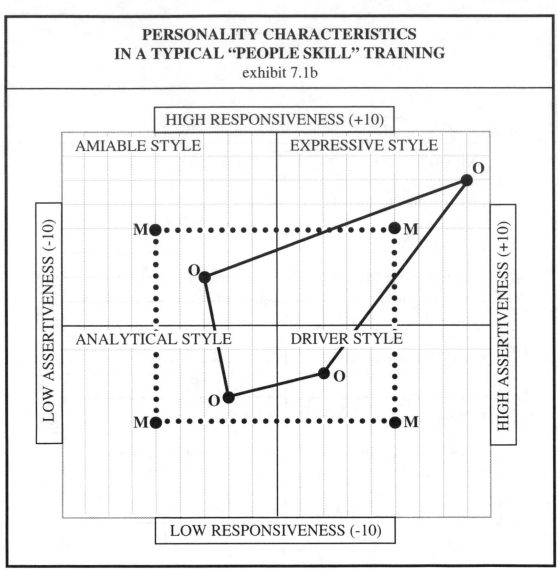

**PERSONALITY CHARACTERISTICS
IN A TYPICAL "PEOPLE SKILL" TRAINING**
exhibit 7.1b

A Course in Miracles in 5 Minutes

Notice that my view of myself, "M" is much more balanced than my view of my opponent, "O". The Course says that the picture I have drawn for my opponent is my real view of myself. He is a reflection of my beliefs, since the world I see is one I created.

On the opposite page is exhibit 7.2b. Complete this exhibit, using 7.1b as a guide. Using "M" for yourself, plot one point in each style area. Then pick one person in your life with whom you have difficulty in relating, and plot that person on the grid as "O". Finally, connect your points as shown in exhibit 7.1b, above.

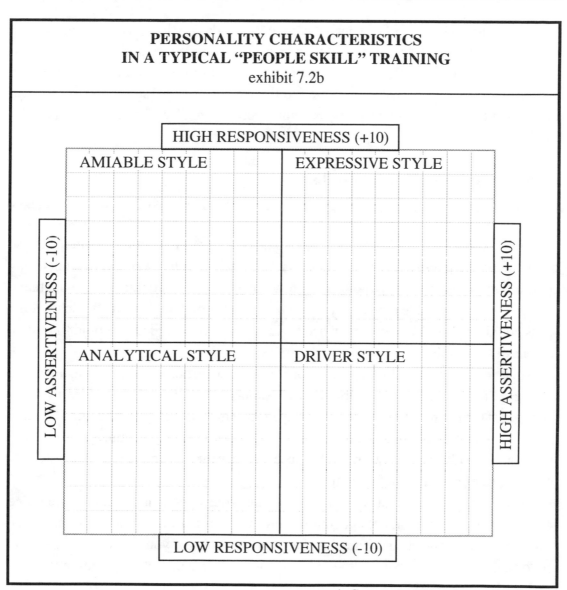

**PERSONALITY CHARACTERISTICS
IN A TYPICAL "PEOPLE SKILL" TRAINING**
exhibit 7.2b

HIGH RESPONSIVENESS (+10)

AMIABLE STYLE   EXPRESSIVE STYLE

LOW ASSERTIVENESS (-10)   HIGH ASSERTIVENESS (+10)

ANALYTICAL STYLE   DRIVER STYLE

LOW RESPONSIVENESS (-10)

A Course in Miracles in 5 Minutes

Now re-read the "solutions" given in each of the four quadrants of exhibit 7a. These solutions are typical of the kinds of recommended actions given in most people-skill trainings.

Take a minute and think about your ability to implement the interpersonal skills solutions given for each of the four personality types in 7a, as you review your markings above.

Now that you have marked your and your opponent's positions, what do you do with it? Most people-skill trainings would then present an elaborate grid of different ways to interact productively with each of these four personality types, similar to the text in exhibit 7a. The idea is that you memorize the actions you are supposed to take and implement them in live interactions, assuming you can modify your own style in order to do this.

Fear blocks using "people skills"

How do you feel about this approach? My own experience, after numerous such trainings, is that I would always revert to my own type. I would also forget what I was supposed to do to "deal" with other personality types. Most often I would get so frightened of, or mad at, the other person that I couldn't or didn't want to implement any conciliatory skills anyway. Of course, my problem didn't have anything to do with them. Rather, I was creating the problem by my own anger. Few of the coldly methodical people skills could help me relate to them when I was so angry or scared that I couldn't remain in control of myself.

Most people are often in the position of having great difficulty overcoming their own feelings. They need to do this first to dispassionately recall, analyze and apply these solutions. That is why the comment is often made that these trainings can be like a Chinese meal. You feel fine immediately after eating, but quickly get hungry again. The information tends not to stay with us because we actively resist or sabotage it, naturally returning our original belief system.

To test this, think about what both your, and your opponent's, belief system and solutions are. Do not look back at your writing. Try to bring to memory that which you just wrote down. The chances are high that your memories of your opponent are so fear and/or anger inducing, that it is the fear and anger you recall, not the solution you just marked down.

The difference in Course versus skill beliefs

A Course in Miracles has a different approach to this problem. It starts with you. The Course theory is that nothing will change until you do. After you change, these "people skills" become simply a way of implementing your belief system. When a proposed action is in battle with your beliefs, there is not much chance that you will successfully implement that action. Exhibit 7c reflects Course beliefs.

PERSONALITY CHARACTERISTICS IN A TYPICAL "PEOPLE-SKILL" TRAINING WITH COURSE SOLUTIONS
exhibit 7c

HIGH RESPONSIVENESS (+10)

LOW ASSERTIVENESS (-10)

AMIABLE STYLE
Likes group interaction,
but is not a good results-
getting leader

solution: he is a HLCG, as
such, he needs my love - if I
give that love, we will both
gain.

EXPRESSIVE STYLE
Likes involvement, but can't
stay focused

solution: this HLCG is a gift to
me since I need to practice pat-
ience and non-confrontational
behavior.

ANALYTICAL STYLE
Cautious, wants data and
firm structure

solution: there is something
I can learn (the gift) from his
slow methodical approach.

DRIVER STYLE
Controlling, but low people
empathy

solution: how lonely it must be
for this HLCG, and how he must
suffer from insecurities. As such,
he is giving me the gift of
showing me how not to do it.

HIGH ASSERTIVENESS (+10)

LOW RESPONSIVENESS (-10)

A Course in Miracles in 5 Minutes

The theme in exhibit 7c is a consistent one of applying three principles of the Course. First, every action is either love or a call for love. Second, every challenge has a gift in it. Finally, everyone is a HLCG, even if they do not realize it. Those three principles apply in every quadrant, with every person, always under all circumstances and always work. Do you feel confident that when you believe in these three Course principles, you will have better relationships with people?

The universality of applying these Course principles is what makes them usable. They may be radical compared to your current thoughts, but look at where your current thoughts have gotten you. If you compare the suggested solutions in the two exhibits, (7a versus 7c) you will see some strong contrasts. For example, compare two solutions: "be specific with a high organization of topics" and "there is something I can learn (the gift) from his slow methodical approach." The first is something you must do whether or not you like it, agree with it, want to do it, can do it, or find it immediately productive. The second is something you do because you agree with it and want to do it. When you feel this way, you will do it and it will be productive.

Applying Course beliefs at home

Our spouse, parents and children are, for many people, the longest running battle-ground of our lives. While they can be a source of continuous conflict, the Course says that they also can be our fastest path to spiritual growth. We all tend to hold, relish and embellish our grievances. Doing this is a way we achieve our separation from God and from the God in our fellow man.

I have, in my own experience, participated in hundreds of incest survivors group meetings. In these meetings I have listened to numerous survivors rail against their perpetrators. These perpetrators were, in most cases, parents, older siblings, aunts, uncles or other older relatives. The least amount of growth and ability to release seems to take place in those people who complain the loudest and longest. These individuals seem to have dedicated themselves to self destruction in order to prove how abused they were.

The Course says that this is just another form of separation from God. If people believe they are separated from God, they will see their lives as a long series of punishments. In their view, they should be punished for being separate. Their perpetrators are only the instruments of that punishment. If the molestation hadn't happened, they would pick other punishers. In fact their principal torturer is themselves. In contrast to this is the simple truth that you cannot punish a holy loving child of God.

Many people tend to carry out this separation punishment in their family life. Thus, in the view of the Course, they seek their own punishment and hell before God can do it to them. Their family lives are a reflection of this mind set and belief system. A result is many lifelong family feuds. Examples are those who grew up together, but no longer "speak"; those who cordially hate each other; those who will "never forget", etc. The Course tells us that none of this is real. It is all of our own creation. The anger, suffering and fighting happens because we see ourselves as other than a holy, loving child of God. My own experience, with my mother's family, is an example. Having immigrated from Italy, they brought with them the traditional Mediterranean tendency for the family vendetta toward one another. It continues to this day.

Do you remember the frontline combat soldier with which we started this chapter? He could see his opposing number as the enemy or as a holy, loving child of God. This is simply another illustration of that principle. A child is most often born into a family with other relatives. Those people may be happy or sad, balanced or crazy, smart or dumb, sensitive or brutish, loving or vindictive, sexually normal or perverted, workers or thieves, etc. The child then becomes subject to these influences, over which he apparently has little control. The constant is that the child can always make one decision. That decision is that he is a HLCG or that he is something else.

It is no different for the combat soldier. He did not overtly elect to go to the front. He generally is not a killer by desire. He had no desire to be put in an environment of killers. He only wants to go home. For either the child or the soldier in such an environment, there is really only one home. That home is the God inside of him. He finds his way home from his belief that there is a loving place, a Father who cares for and about him, no matter what his current environment.

In this sense both the child and the soldier have many things in common. They are both controlled by outside forces that do not have spiritual agendas. Both the child and the soldier need help. Neither is likely to get it from this world. Both the child's family and the soldier's country are at war. Both soldier and child become simply an implement to carry out that war. As such, there is no recognition of the HLCG within them. They become their controller's (family or country) pawns in wars in which they are unwilling participants. The more severe the circumstance, the greater the gift. They should be able to see themselves as strong, capable, pure, loving children of God. When they see this, they are able to rise above the insanity that surrounds them. Which is to say, they may be in this world, but they are not of it.

The soldier at least has buddies with whom to do a reality check. The child is generally alone, without experience or comrades for reality checking. If you were in such a position, as a child, it is now you (as an adult) who has to take the steps to relate to your family. You cannot have a decent relationship so long as you continue to hold grudges for your mistreatment. The holding of the grudge is, in itself, the denial of your, and their, being HLCG. As long as you deny this, you will continue to be in pain.

My own experience

I mentioned my own loving, fighting, hating mother's Italian family. It is a fine example of feuds that had gone on for decades. Little or nothing changed, until I did. Then the changes were dramatic. For example, I could be bitter to this day toward them about being packed off to "Christian" schools were I was continuously attacked, beaten, raped, and otherwise emotionally abused. I could further be even more enraged because this abuse was done as a result of my being "Jewish", even though I really didn't know what a Jew was. My anger could even be deeper when I think of the frustration of having nowhere to turn: no father, an absent mother, no available relatives, no protector. My anger would easily turn to rage when I thought of spending my life being afraid that someone would discover my "Jewishness" and kill me.

I never really had peace on the issue until I forgave my family and the priests, monks, teachers and older boys for the molestations and beatings. Having been the subject of this and endless childhood death threats in these "Christian" schools because of my Jewish father, I could easily be bitter and vindictive. The Course would say that the longevity (ages 8 to 14) of this experience and its intensity (weekly and in some cases daily) marks the importance of the gift.

Does this idea of a gift seem strange to you? The gift was that I had, under extreme circumstances as a child, the opportunity to see myself as a HLCG. The now famous writings of Victor Frankl in Nazi concentration camps mirror this experience. Peace came to him from within. Because of my extreme position of being alone as a child, with no protection and no one with whom to identify, my experience could have given me a great self identity. At least Jews in the concentration camps had other Jews with whom to relate. A "Jew" in a right wing Christian school is like a mouse in the cat's den. In this sense, I had a marvelous opportunity, but I was not equal to it.

Looking at your own family in Course terms

The Course has two cornerstones. They are love and forgiveness. It can be hard to tell where one starts and the other ends. If you continue to hate, in Course terms, you only hate yourself, because what you see and feel is a mirror of yourself. You cannot believe that you are a HLCG and believe that others should be hated since they are not HLCG. Your history, with your family of origin, tends to have more emotionalism than anything else in your life. Because of this, we are going to take a detailed look at your family–from both a worldly, and a Course perspective.

Following is exhibit 7d which asks you to simply take a look at the three most significant problems and gifts in your relationship(s) with your family. You will be asked to identify them yourself, since no one else can do this for you. Then we will show one person's worldly response (mine) in exhibit 7e and a Course response in exhibit 7f.

As usual, your best benefit will come from not looking ahead before completing exhibit 7d. The ranking, or grading, system to be used is the same one as in other exhibits: from -10 to 0 to +10. If have any questions about this rankings system, remember it is explained in Chapter 1. You may not be able to list all the things that you like or dislike about your family. That is OK, just try to list the ones most important to you.

THREE THINGS I LIKE LEAST AND BEST ABOUT MY FAMILY
exhibit 7d

Rank your feelings from -10 (strongly disagree) to +10 (strongly agree).
If you can't rank your feelings, leave them unranked.

A. I don't like these things about the way my family functions:	B. I don't like them because:	Rank -10 to +10
1.		
2.		
3.		
B. I do like these things about the way my family functions:	B. I do like them because:	
1.		
2.		
3.		

Did you find that it was easier to think of things you didn't like rather than those you did? You may well also find that the intensity of your feelings about your dislikes is stronger than about your likes. Many people find that this is the case. Of course, it is difficult to relate to your family if you are carrying a lot of high-intensity feelings from the past. The Course tells us that these negative feelings have in them many gifts. One of these gifts is the ability to get over those negative feelings.

To illustrate how negative we can get, I have completed exhibit 7d for myself. It is shown on the following page as exhibit 7e.

THREE THINGS I LIKE LEAST AND BEST ABOUT MY FAMILY
exhibit 7e - An example of my own reactions to my family.

Rank your feelings from -10 (strongly disagree) to +10 (strongly agree).
If you can't rank your feelings, leave them unranked.

A. I don't like these things about the way my family functions:	B. I don't like them because:	Rank -10 to +10
1. *They are uneducated and show it. Their subjects, conversation, and mannerisms are uninformed.*	*It reminds me of how much I was denied as a child.*	+4
2. *They are always fighting. Their gripes go on for decades. Their grudges are repeated endlessly.*	*I never learned how to love and forgive rather than fight.*	+6
3. *They have little or no ambition. As a result their lives are a dull repetitive endless routine.*	*I am terrified at the possibility of having such a life.*	+8
B. I do like these things about the way my family functions:	B. I do like them because:	
1. *They truly forgive me for not being in contact with them for two decades.*	*They have taught me a real lesson in forgiveness and love.*	+9
2. *They had their own set of problems. Actually, they dealt with them pretty well.*	*They show that one can adjust to all kinds of conditions.*	+4
3. *Their ongoing battles show me how I could do lots better. They still are at it, a great lesson.*	*They show me the energy that could be in love versus hate.*	+5

A Course in Miracles in 5 Minutes

I am in my 50s. My aunts and uncles are in their 70s. How would they react if they knew my feelings? Probably in the same ways that I have described in this exhibit. Suffice to say that, if they read this, I may not have a family any more. Notice my rankings of my feelings. I gave A1 a +4. Only a few years ago, prior to being in the Course, that +4 would have been a +10.

My +6 ranking for A2 reflects my ego at work. Compare this to my +5 ranking to B3. Thus, their battles are a problem for me, if I make it so. As a child, I could have known that there was something wrong here (without knowing what). Had I made this decision I would have looked on their fighting as a great example of what not to do (B3). I did not have this view as a child and, as a result, became subject myself to the same hostility and anger that they were exhibiting. This shows in my +6 ranking to A2.

The nutritionists tell us we are what we eat. The Course would say we are what we think. To illustrate this, following is exhibit 7f, completed to show how these same problems would be looked at from a Course perspective.

A COURSE IN MIRACLES PERSPECTIVE ABOUT
THREE THINGS I LIKE LEAST AND BEST ABOUT MY FAMILY
exhibit 7f

Rank your feelings from -10 (strongly disagree) to +10 (strongly agree).
If you can't rank your feelings, leave them unranked.

A. I don't like these things about the way my family functions:	B. I don't like them because:	Rank -10 to +10
1. *They are uneducated and show it. Their subjects, conversation, and mannerisms are uninformed.*	*High or low class is my ego speaking. They are HLCG.*	+7
2. *They are always fighting. Their gripes go on for decades. Their grudges are repeated endlessly.*	*What a marvelous gift to see first hand anger versus love.*	+6
3. *They have little or no ambition. As a result their lives are a dull repetitive endless routine.*	*This life has only one goal, to reach atonement with God.*	+8
B. I do like these things about the way my family functions:	B. I do like them because:	
1. *They truly forgive me for not being in contact with them for two decades.*	*I should only be as good as they are in forgiving and love.*	+9
2. *They had their own set of problems. Actually, they dealt with them pretty well.*	*Knowing that we all struggle with our egos, I see theirs.*	+6
3. *Their ongoing battles show me how I could do lots better. They still are at it, a great lesson.*	*"All things are lessons I would learn" (Course)*	+8

Do you notice the road to Course beliefs is to look at the positive side of your prior complaints? Notice that the answers to the "B" statements are close to Course beliefs. The only real difference is that the "B" statements in exhibit 7f are the most spiritual. The difference between being positive and being a Course student is basically the source of those beliefs. There are many positive people who were simply brought up with a positive belief system. They may, or may not, have a spiritual belief system.

For those who were given, or adopted, a negative belief system, the Course can be particularly helpful. In the Course, you start early to disassemble your negative beliefs. For example, Lesson 23 says, "When you finally learn that thoughts of attack and being attacked are not different you will be ready to let the cause go." Lesson 24 says, "I do not perceive my own best interests". Lesson 25 says, "Everything is for your own best interests. That is what it is for; that is its purpose; that is what it means."

When you believe these kinds of statements, your life changes automatically. The trick is to get to the point of believing them. To help you on this journey, turn back to the question about the front line combat soldier, posed at the beginning of this chapter. Put yourself back to the time when you were a child facing the issues you have outlined in exhibit 7d. How many times did you then fear for your life, and/or wish to "kill" your relatives or parents? Would you, with the wisdom of an adult, do it today?

Chapter 8

The Miracle of Healing the Blind Beggar

T he miracle we are seeking is far more important than merely the conversion of water to wine. It is, in every sense, the healing of the blind beggar. That unfortunate sightless, fearful, limited person is us. We are blind about being surrounded by love. We beg for that which is already ours in abundance.

The steps to healing the blind beggar are simple, but they are not easy. To help remember them, they are set out in the next four exhibits, which have been designed for you to copy and carry with you as individual cards. The first card outlines what we need to overcome. The second card shows the results we get. The third card has the path to do it. The fourth, and final, card shows how the Course helps us to get it done. Use each card for a week, then rotate it for the next card.

The Course in a nutshell
(or at least in four exhibits)

In order to heal the blind beggar, most of us need to overcome three obstacles. Reminding ourselves of these obstacles to peace will help to bring us back from the insanity of this world to our spiritual peace.

OBSTACLES TO BE OVERCOME
(exhibit 8a)

1. what I have been brought up to believe, I am,
2. the insanity of this world tends to reinforces my limited belief, and
3. my religious training, if it supports a God who can be or has been angry or vengeful, at any time–ever.

A Course in Miracles in 5 Minutes

The Course shows us the results we can get from this most important miracle of all–our own healing. There are three results. Use them to measure your progress.

THREE STEPS IN MEASURING MY PROGRESS
(exhibit 8b)

1. my self beliefs change to seeing myself as a holy, loving child of God,
2. the world may remain just as insane, but is it not insane for me, and
3. I understand that it is me, not God, who created this insane world.

A Course in Miracles in 5 Minutes

Our beliefs undergo these dramatic changes because we see ourselves and our brothers in a different way. These changes in perception are, perhaps, our most difficult challenge. We need regular reminders of our new view.

MY NEW VIEW OF MY WORLD
(exhibit 8c)

1. Every action I, or they, take is either love or a call for love, both of which need the response of love.
2. I know that my life is controlled by my beliefs and by the thoughts that result from them.
3. My "problems" are my gifts, and as such, I look for the message about me in each problem, knowing I created the problem and made my own world.

A Course in Miracles in 5 Minutes

We use the Course to achieve this miracle of healing the blind beggar. The Course is simply the road map of a spiritual journey we must make. We know that others may choose a different road map or journey. Because our own trip is a spiritual journey, we neither oppose nor endorse the journey that others may take. We are glad that they are on any path toward a reconciliation with the God within them. We look forward to not encountering them as a blind beggar while we are also trying to move along our own road. We do not want to sit beside the road as a blind beggar ourselves. Our only desire is that each of us get to the destination. As such, we keep reminding ourselves of three important facets of the Course, shown in exhibit 8d.

IN USING THE COURSE ROAD MAP, I BELIEVE
(exhibit 8d)

1. it is one of a thousand paths, all equally good. I do not condemn my brother for his path.
2. it is a complete belief system that I can use to substitute for my insane view of an insane world.
3. it is the path that gives me the most peace. I know, by my loss of peace, when I wander off of it.

A Course in Miracles in 5 Minutes

Is the journey worth the trouble
(or should I not make the trip)?

We should remind ourselves about the purpose of all of the energy that we put into this journey. The Course makes two key promises. Those promises are that: 1. if we have "a little willingness", God will do the rest, and 2. if we embrace this belief in a loving God, we will experience an abundance of joy and peace.

This peace is not a reward tossed to us from God for being good girls and boys. Rather, it is the natural result of being comfortable with ourselves and our relationship to God. In traditional Christianity it is called grace. However, the "grace" of traditional religion has an inherent conflict. It requires that we believe in a God with the capacity for both anger and wrath.

Our belief in a loving God enables us to call on Him/Her when we are confused as to the right answer. That confusion happens often in this insane world. We then truly become one of the few who sees the insanity of everything, except love, in this world. Thus, when we are faced with the most common dilemmas from work, marriage, or any other close relationship, we need only ask one question: Which decision is the closest to the expression of a loving God?

The commitment required in this Course journey has two benefits. The first benefit is to get us to believe enough to be able to ask the same threshold question each time we are challenged. That question is: What is the love in this challenge? The second benefit is to be able to figure out the answer.

In Course terms this is "a journey without a distance", because we never really left the home of our God. Since we have simply created the separation, we have the power to end it. When we distanced ourselves from God, we built our fears which keep that separation. The greatest fear of which is that an angry God will punish us for our unforgivable "sins". We then try to beat Him to the punch by punishing ourselves.

How do we overcome these gigantic fears? In the same way, as some wag said, as we eat an elephant—one bite at a time. These "bites" of experience in dealing with fears will enable us to mix some positive results with our academic understanding. Taking a chance (like eating the first few bites) is the most difficult. My own experience is that once having eaten parts of that "elephant of a fear", eating the rest is easier. Eating the second and third elephants are easiest.

For example, remember the story of my own childhood persecution. It caused me to believe the insanity taught to me: that if anyone discovered that my father was Jewish,

I would be killed. Well, I have disclosed that to the world, and I am still here. It only took me 52 years. It should have taken 52 minutes.

How much time will it take for you to expose the insanity of your fears? I will use my situation as an example. As a child I was taught, from both the pulpit and the bed, by both Catholic priests and Protestant ministers that, because I was Jewish, I deserved to suffer. This "teaching" was given in both sermons and "personal instruction." I was also taught a fundamental belief system of traditional religions: That God is capable of anger. To a child locked in an institutional setting, this is the word of God. Therefore: 1) God is angry and vengeful, especially to "sinners," 2) the Jews committed the worst sin of all, they killed Christ, and therefore 3) my only escape was not to be "Jewish". I took too much time to test the fear. Even though all three of these teachings are insane, they were backed by repeated sexual molestation and beatings, causing much childhood pain and fear. The result was the same as any other torture inflicted on a child. Eventually, it is possible to produce in a child much of that which is sought.

When you want to discover your driving fears, look at your own childhood. It may not be as dramatic as mine. At least I hope it is not. However, you know how much pain you are experiencing. That pain comes from your fears. Your fears arise from your beliefs. How long will it take you to overcome your beliefs that give rise to your fears, which cause your pain?

Plotting yourself on exhibit 8e will help you to answer these questions. As with some similar prior exhibits, the purpose of 8e is to give you a convenient outline to think through these difficult personal questions. If you are doing this with others, (ie: in a Course in Miracles group setting) there is a real advantage in sharing your "secrets." By completing 8e, you can more readily address important issues. How much time will it take for you to "cure" these fears? The answer is in two questions. How motivated are you? What is your threshold for pain?

The ranking scale is the same as in all other exhibits. In this exhibit, use the line above each of the three scales (beliefs, fears and pain) to jot down your most significant problem. The lines below may be used for notes to yourself. As usual, do not look ahead before completing exhibit 8e as well as you can.

MY BELIEF, FEAR, PAIN SCALE
(exhibit 8e)

Rank yourself by using -10 as the most negative, 0 as neutral and +10 as the most positive. Use the line above the ranking scale to identify your most difficult issue. The lines below may be used for notes to yourself.

BELIEFS

My most crippling belief: _____

|————————————————|————————————————|
-10   0   +10

_____

_____

_____

_____

FEARS

My greatest fear: _____

|————————————————|————————————————|
-10   0   +10

_____

_____

_____

_____

PAIN

My most recurring pain: _____

|————————————————|————————————————|
-10   0   +10

_____

_____

_____

_____

It may be difficult to place your fears into a mild (0 to +10) category if your beliefs are very negative. Similarly, you will not ease your pain if you are full of highly negative fears. This is one of the reasons the Course can be so effective. It gives us a whole new belief system. The Course tells us that we create our own world, by our beliefs. We are therefore a manifestation of our worst fears.

The Course solution to the belief-fear-pain cycle

The degree of anger or withdrawal that you experience in your life is a good indicator of the amount of negativity you have in these three categories. The Course is clear that a holy, loving child of God cannot be angry. There is nothing to be angry about. Therefore, the further you are from God, the more angry you will be. Your feelings of separation and abandonment lead to your anger. If you have the courage, ask some people who know you, who you really are. Then, trust them to tell you honestly how angry they believe you to be.

This is a difficult self examination. You can ask your friends or group members for feedback or ideas. To illustrate, I will use my own situation, which may be extreme. I hope you are able to put it to use, as it is relative to you. In exhibit 8f, I have marked two places on each scale. The first mark is a "T" for then. The "then" means before I started in the Course. I have also marked a "N" for now. I honestly believe that these differences are due to my work in the Course.

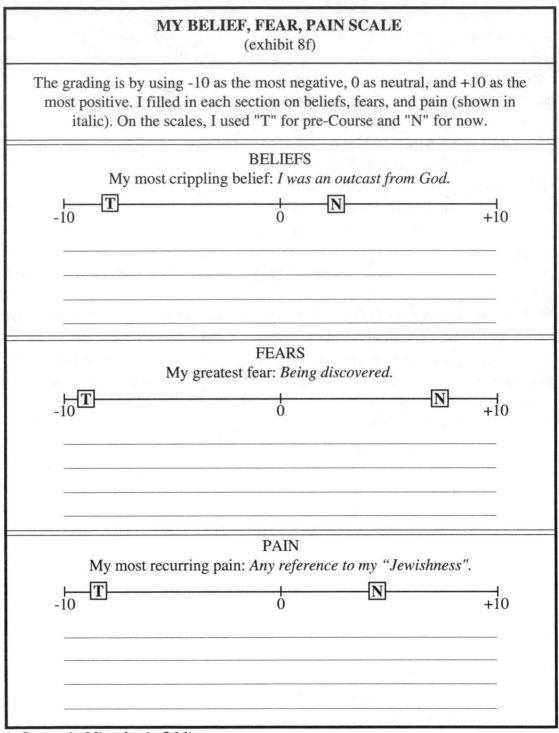

MY BELIEF, FEAR, PAIN SCALE
(exhibit 8f)

The grading is by using -10 as the most negative, 0 as neutral, and +10 as the most positive. I filled in each section on beliefs, fears, and pain (shown in italic). On the scales, I used "T" for pre-Course and "N" for now.

BELIEFS
My most crippling belief: *I was an outcast from God.*

T		N	
-10	0		+10

_____

_____

_____

FEARS
My greatest fear: *Being discovered.*

T		N	
-10	0		+10

_____

_____

_____

PAIN
My most recurring pain: *Any reference to my "Jewishness".*

T		N	
-10	0		+10

_____

_____

_____

You may well think that my crippling belief, fear and pain is silly. Of course, you are right. There is anti-Semitism in the United States, and lots of it in some areas. However, there has not been a Jew murdered in the U.S. for being Jewish in more than 100 years. This is the case in even the most bigoted of big cities and rural areas. Having been raised as a Christian, and having a non-Jewish mother, I probably wouldn't qualify as a Jew anyway, even among Jews. It doesn't make any difference. That fear has still controlled most of my life.

Now, look at your belief, fear, and pain. It may be difficult for you to be as objective about your own fears as you can be about mine. If you are having this objectivity struggle, I suggest that you reread the section about the Course and openness. Basically, what the Course says is that all such fears are a result of our belief that we are separated from God. I could not fear death if I believed I was a HLCG. Trace your fear to the underlying belief. You will find that your belief at its core is always the same. You believe that you are separated from God.

It does not matter whether you believe that the separation is because God: 1) doesn't exist, 2) doesn't care, 3) is angry, 4) has more important issues, 5) abandoned you or 6) is punishing you. In the Course, these objections all have the same answer. God exists as a timeless all-loving creator. You have separated yourself from God. He is incapable of anger, punishment, abandonment or any other worldly emotion. We place these worldly emotions on Him as part of our separation. We created the separation. We give it life and we continue it.

When you look at your fears, they can only come from a belief in separation. If you believed in a loving God who wants you as a HLCG, by definition you could have no fears. When you carry that belief to this insane world, you will see that problems in this world are therefore but gifts to a HLCG.

Your problems are your gifts

You will recall that we did a number of earlier exercises about our view of the world. The result of those exercises is always the same. The world we experience is the one we create. The Course tells us that we can control our world by controlling our thoughts. If you continue to have doubts about this, try a quick exercise.

Think first about the most loving person or thing in your life and plan to do something with them. Stop and fix this in your mind. Now think about your single greatest fear. Stop and fix this in your mind. What was it you planned to do in love? The answer is either very difficult to remember, or can't be remembered at all. Your mind has controlled your reality.

The Course tells us that our problems are a mirror reflection of our beliefs. To test this, try completing exhibit 8g. List your five toughest problems. Include anything that is making your life difficult. These problems do not have to be in any order of difficulty. Indeed, the Course tells us that there is no order of difficulty. All problems are the same. As with all other exhibits in this book, do not look ahead.

A LIST OF MY FIVE MOST DIFFICULT PROBLEMS
exhibit 8g

List your 5 most difficult problems in any order.

1. _____
   _____
   _____
   _____
   _____

2. _____
   _____
   _____
   _____
   _____

3. _____
   _____
   _____
   _____
   _____

4. _____
   _____
   _____
   _____
   _____

5. _____
   _____
   _____
   _____
   _____

Now, take those five most difficult problems and try to figure out what the gift is in them. Remember that the Course promises us that each one is a gift. If it is a problem with a person, look at what it is about that person you do not like. This is the issue that you have with yourself. In short, it is a part of yourself that you like least. You aren't highly troubled if someone stutters, unless you are worried about your own speech patterns.

It won't anger you if someone is late, sloppy, lazy, hostile, rejecting, abrupt or vengeful unless you are projecting that as a behavior of your own. In Course view, we project, as just described, or we extend. To extend means to extend the love of God. We cannot both project and extend at the same time. Our projections show us when we are not extending.

If you think that your problems are "things" rather than people, the same rules apply. Most people spend their lives either in want and worry or in comfort and joy. The difference is not what they have, but rather what they perceive that they have. We have talked about, and will further deal with, the Course and money. Since we, not God, put us here, He can hardly be expected to stick a few bucks in our bank account. Completing both exhibit 8g and 8h should help you see how both your people and things problems result from your projections.

You can now list what the Course would call the reverse side of your problems. These are the gifts from your "problems." We will therefore list them as gifts. Listing problems as gifts is so foreign to most people that you may not be able to do it. If you are unable to, you have a special dispensation to look ahead at exhibits 8i and 8j. These are completed examples. It would, however, be better if you tried as hard as possible to complete exhibit 8h before looking ahead.

A LIST OF MY GIFTS ARISING OUT OF MY FEARS
exhibit 8h

List your 5 most important gifts arising out of the problems in exhibit 8g. Put them in the same order.

1. _____
_____
_____
_____
_____

2. _____
_____
_____
_____
_____

3. _____
_____
_____
_____
_____

4. _____
_____
_____
_____
_____

5. _____
_____
_____
_____
_____

Were you able to do it? If so, congratulations! If not, try one more time before looking ahead. Consider the first problem that you have listed in Exhibit 8g. Then think about why that problem troubles you. What is your underlying fear? When you have identified your fear, try to find the belief on which your fear is based. Remember that the Course is clear that our problems always flow from our fears and that our fears always flow from our beliefs.

If you can't find your underlying fear and belief in the problem you listed first, then go to each of your four other problems in order and try the same process. It is important to keep in mind that there is never any reason for projection except fear. If you keep thinking about it, you will probably come up with your fear and belief for each of the five problems. Sleep on it. Talk to your group, friend or spouse about it. You will find it!

As promised, here is an example of five problems. The problems in this exhibit (8i) are mine.

A LIST OF MY PROBLEMS
exhibit 8i

A list of my five most difficult problems, not in any order.

1. I watch for rejection so I can cut them off quickly.
2. Because I look so Jewish I am sensitive to discrimination.
3. I am invested in money, so I give it undue importance.
4. I am still on my search for the father I didn't have.
5. I am jealous of women. They have it a lot easier.

A Course in Miracles in 5 Minutes

As you can see, I still suffer from beliefs arising out of my childhood incest and abuse. As a child, being sensitive to rejection was, in my belief, a matter of life and death. I went to bed many nights with death threats: "You will be killed in your sleep during the night". Therefore, it was crucial to identify who was friend or foe. To be Jewish meant to be harassed and killed. Therefore, I could never be myself. Of course, the irony was that I was not Jewish, only looked it. I still wonder what people are thinking.

My only imagined protection was money. As a poor child, having money meant being safe. Therefore, I invested money with so much power that it became an unachievable goal. It was like a God, to be worshiped, but never really achieved because of my low self esteem. Since my father abandoned me, I couldn't be worth much. Therefore, I am always on the lookout for mentoring older men (there aren't many left who are older) who can be a father substitute.

My childhood fantasy was that if I were a girl, I would have lots of advantages. I wouldn't: 1) be subject to physical attacks, 2) have to defend myself, 3) be sexually molested, 4) be abandoned by my father, 5) be so subject to persecution for being Jewish (I changed my name as a kid as soon as I could scrape the few bucks together for the filing fees). Of course, none of this is reality. Girls are raped, molested, attacked, abandoned and persecuted, just as I was. My illusion was that society protects girls, but not boys. Of course, this probably had most to do with being in boys' schools.

We all make these childhood survival decisions. They form our beliefs. To the extent that we feel abandoned, our beliefs can cause desperate behavior, as did mine. The fact that these beliefs are irrational makes no difference. I hope that your circumstances and beliefs are not as extreme as mine. But, for purposes of Course teachings, it doesn't make any difference. I will illustrate this by showing the impact of the Course in changing these from problems to gifts. In reading these, remember that I have not solved all of these problems completely. There are still lots of residuals but, while still working to eliminate them, my life has become a lot easier. I still waver between the beliefs shown in exhibits 8i and 8j. Each year I get closer to the beliefs shown in exhibit 8j.

A LIST OF MY GIFTS ARISING OUT OF MY FEARS
exhibit 8j
A list of my 5 most important gifts in the same order as 8i.
1. A HLCG cannot be rejected. Rejection reminds me of this. 2. Rejection for my Race saves me time by eliminating bigots. 3. I cannot love worldly things and God at the same time. 4. My gift is knowing I have the best Father possible. 5. The gift is the reminder-God knows no gender differences.

A Course in Miracles in 5 Minutes

Your final task on the road to being a HLCG

After you have completed this exercise, you will probably find it helpful to try something similar to this on a weekly basis. Shown below, in exhibit 8k, is a sample section of "Worksheet For Applying Course Principles To Problems." The page following this is a blank worksheet (exhibit 8l) which you can copy and use. This worksheet enables you to organize your reactions in four major areas of your life: family, social, work and "other." For each section, jot down the problem, your fear, the course message or gift, and how to apply the gift.

			COURSE MESSAGE OR GIFT	
AREA	MY PROBLEM	MY FEAR	WHAT IT IS	APPLYING IT
F A M I L Y	Having once been abandoned, can I now get close to my family without running the risk again? This results in my ambivalent feelings toward my family.	The fear of being abandoned runs deep. It was such a lonely feeling as a child. I don't want it again.	As a holy loving child of God, I cannot be abandoned. I carry God with me. I can abandon Him, but He will never abandon me.	Whenever I am with my family I remember that the strength I have does not come from them. They are a gift in reminding me that my source is not of this world.

WORKSHEET FOR APPLYING COURSE PRINCIPLES TO PROBLEMS
exhibit 8k

A Course in Miracles in 5 Minutes

Now, you try it! The entire next page has this complete (exhibit 8l) form ready for you to complete. As usual, do not look ahead.

WORSHEET FOR APPLYING COURSE PRINCIPLES TO PROBLEMS exhibit 81				
AREA	MY PROBLEM	MY FEAR	COURSE MESSAGE OR GIFT WHAT IT IS	APPLYING IT
F A M I L Y				
S O C I A L				
W O R K				
O T H E R				

A Course in Miracles in 5 Minutes

If you couldn't complete exhibit 8l, try it one more time. Then, look at exhibit 8m, which is my completed worksheet. We all probably have a number of "problems" in each of the four categories. It doesn't make any difference which one of yours you pick. Any problem serves that same purpose. After you complete a few worksheets, you will see that your questions tend to be, and the answer is always the same.

| | | | COURSE MESSAGE OR GIFT | |
AREA	MY PROBLEM	MY FEAR	WHAT IT IS	APPLYING IT
F A M I L Y	When my family fights, I don't understand how they can be so negative and still have any relationship left. It scares me to see both their volatility and their anger.	By the time they vent their anger, there will not be any relationship left. I fear that we will abandon each other.	There are two messages here. First, anger is a call for love. Respond with love. Second, I can not be abandoned. A HLCG has, within him, a family.	When I am angry, or getting anger from someone else, I need to continualy remind myself that this is a call for love and give love. Second, I can have only one separation.
S O C I A L	I am so rejection sensitive that I sometimes create it by anticipating it. My lack of self esteem causes me to behave in negative ways which make people withdraw.	If you knew who I am, you would not have anything to do with me.	Who I really am is a HLCG. As such, you will love me as much as you love yourself. The reverse is also true. I cannot love you more than I love myself.	I need to work on loving myself since I can't receive love if I can't give it. My goal is to be able to be in this world, but not of it. Then I can see insanity in an unemotional way.
W O R K	Asking for money is really hard. My self image is of money. When money is an issue, I get so anxious that I can't function. As a result, I often get less than I should.	If I ask for a fair fee or wage, you will attack me. I am so vulnerable that such an attack is too painful.	Money is of this world. If I'm not invested in it, no one will be able to use it against me. Money issues are minimal if I am a HLCG.	So much of my life has focused on a lack of money that I have created a self fulfilling prophesy. I will have enough when it is no longer an issue. Keep reminding myself.
O T H E R	The "glories" of this world have real attraction to me. I like being important. "Importance" has advantages of deference, etc. But I also know it has no meaning.	If I am not "important", I am nobody. If people listen to me, I must be smart. I don't have to consider my issues.	The importance I have is not of this world. Anything and everything of this world has no importance. If I give them importance I am withdrawing from God.	I need to ask myself, about everything: what is it for? This reminder helps me to bring everything back into perspective. I ask myself, would I trade money for God?

A Course in Miracles in 5 Minutes

Do not let the story of the blind beggar be your life. Arise, pick up your worksheets and change your beliefs!

The End

Index

A

a lack of money 129
abandonment 117, 119
acceptance 30, 33, 34, 36, 38, 62, 84
achievements 39, 42
actions 58, 64-69, 71-73, 97, 98, 126
Adams, Henry 83
agnostic 7
AIDS 18
anger viii, ix, x, xi, 1, 2, 15-20, 22-25, 28, 46-48, 50, 52, 55, 58, 61, 64, 80, 92, 98,
    101, 102, 107, 108, 114, 115, 117, 119, 122, 129
anger versus joy 22, 24, 25
angry God ix, x, 19, 47, 48, 114
anti-Semitism 119
appease the gods 34, 39
approval 30, 47, 52
Aquinas, St.Thomas 83
Aristotle 82, 84
atheist 6, 7
atonement 12, 13, 21, 55, 59, 108
attack 9, 25, 43, 53, 58, 60, 64-66, 92, 102, 109, 125, 129
aunt 59, 100, 107
average scores 10, 88

B

balance 63, 65, 66, 88, 96, 101
Balzac 82, 84
battleground of our lives 100
behavior ix, 12, 16, 43, 48, 51, 59, 60, 62, 64, 65, 74, 76, 77, 80, 92, 93, 99, 122, 125
behavioral styles 93
being positive 109
belief v, vii, viii, ix, x, 1-12, 15-24, 26, 28, 31, 32, 34-36, 38-48, 52, 53, 54, 57, 60-75, 79,
    80, 82, 84, 86, 88, 91-94, 96, 98, 100, 101, 109, 112-120, 124, 125, 130
    belief changes 69, 71, 93
    belief in a loving God 24, 114
    belief system vii, viii, x, 1-3, 5-8, 10-12, 18, 19, 21, 22, 24, 31, 32, 34-36, 41, 47, 52,
        59, 60, 62, 63, 65, 70, 80, 92, 93, 98, 101, 109, 113, 115, 117
benchmarks 88

best interest 109
Bible 2, 6, 8, 18, 52
bigot 51, 53, 72, 85, 119, 125
    bigoted 72, 119
    bigotry 51, 53, 72, 85
Biology of Hope 21
blind beggar 111, 113, 130
blocks 98
boss 34, 59, 92
brother x, xi, 12, 26, 59, 71-73, 75, 85, 89, 90, 92, 93, 112, 113
business viii, 1, 44, 54, 72, 74, 92
Butler, Samuel 83

C

call for love 19, 53, 60, 64, 65, 93, 100, 113, 129
cancer 21, 93
cancer treatment center 21
car dealership 67
Catholic viii, ix, 16, 21, 34, 72, 115
change x, 2, 5-10, 15, 17-20, 22, 28, 31, 33, 35, 36, 38, 39, 54, 62, 63, 65, 66-69, 71-73, 75, 77, 79, 80, 84-86, 88-90, 92-94, 98, 102, 109, 112, 125, 130
    change your actions 68
    change your beliefs 15, 68, 130
    changes in perception 112
child viii, ix, x, 11, 12, 16, 18, 22, 25, 30, 32, 36, 38, 42-45, 51-54, 59, 67, 71, 72, 75, 77, 79, 80, 84, 90, 92, 94, 100-102, 106, 107, 109, 112, 114, 115, 117, 124-126
child molesters 52
childhood viii, x, 16, 18, 42-45, 52, 80, 84, 102, 114, 115, 124, 125
    childhood message 18, 80
    childhood programming 45
Chinese meal 98
Christ ix, 51, 85, 89, 90, 115
Cicero 83, 84
clever 93
cliques 72
closed 17, 20, 44, 75, 78, 80, 88, 115
Cooper, George Fenimore 82
co-worker 59, 92
combat fighter 92
commitment 24, 88, 114
concentration camp 102
conciliatory skills 98
control 5, 6, 10-13, 16-18, 21, 50, 58, 64, 67, 76, 80, 98, 99, 101, 113, 119, 120
    control our world 119
    controlling our thoughts 119

corrupt 8, 43, 51, 53
counter-attack 92
counting to ten 59
Course in Miracles 1, 3, 7, 8, 17, 20, 35, 75, 84, 91, 92, 115
    Course in Miracles group 115
Cousins, Norman 21

D

Dante 83, 84
death ix, 18, 43, 67, 93, 102, 119, 124
defense ix, 8, 51-53, 92, 93
defenseless ix, 51, 52, 53
denial 28, 102
dependency 8, 72, 73
depression 93
difficult people 59
Diogenes 83, 85
divinity 46, 47
divorce viii, 72
doctor 34, 39, 67
Dostoevsky 84
doubts 90, 119
driving fears 115
Dryden, John 83
Durrell 83, 85

E

ease your pain 117
easy life 11
education 11, 27, 29, 30, 43
ego viii, x, 6, 16, 52, 55, 59, 66, 77, 92, 93, 107, 108
Einstein, Albert 30, 83
employed by God 30, 71
employee 34, 59, 92
employment firings 72
enemy 67, 92, 93, 101
evil x, 6, 15, 93
exhibits *see Directory of Exhibits in the front of this book*
exclusion 72
extend 122

F

faith 5, 7, 9-11, 16

family viii, ix, 72, 101-108, 126, 129
    family feuds 101
    family functions 104, 106, 108
Father (God) 125
father viii, x, 12, 16, 51, 59, 101, 102, 114, 124, 125
fear ix, x, xi, 6, 16, 18, 19, 28, 55, 59, 67, 75-79, 89, 90, 98, 109, 114-119, 124, 126, 127, 129
fears 6, 11, 16, 17, 19, 20, 52, 75-78, 89, 90, 92, 114-119, 123-125
feedback 117
feelings 2, 3, 7, 15-17, 20, 24, 26, 28, 29, 32, 33, 61, 63, 64, 72, 77, 79, 80-82, 85, 87, 89, 98, 104-108, 117
festering 65
five toughest problems 120
Ford, Henry 83
forgive ix, x, 106, 108
forgiveness ix, 34, 75, 103, 106
Frankl, Victor 102

G

gift x, 9, 10, 15, 25-27, 29, 30, 59, 61, 62, 64, 66, 71, 88, 99-102, 108, 122, 125-127, 129
gifts x, 18, 43, 48, 75, 88, 103, 105, 113, 119, 122, 123, 125
God viii, ix, x, 1, 2, 6-8, 11, 12, 16, 18-24, 30, 32, 34, 36, 38, 39, 43, 45, 47, 48, 52, 54, 55, 59, 61, 67, 71-73, 75, 77, 79, 81, 82, 84, 85, 87, 89, 90, 92, 94, 100, 101, 108, 112-115, 117-119, 122, 125, 126, 129
    God within 113
good deeds 35, 73
government 72
grace 114
grievances 46, 100
guru 32, 34, 47
gurus 48

H

happy relationships 59
hard work 11, 85, 89, 90
hate 81, 82, 84, 85, 89, 90, 101, 103, 106
healing the blind beggar 111, 113
health 93
heart failure 93
hell 6, 11, 101
higher self esteem 54
Hitler 8
HLCG 12, 16, 20, 22, 30, 52, 54, 59-61, 63-65, 67, 68, 71-75, 78, 79, 89, 93, 99-103, 108, 119, 125, 126, 129

holy, loving child of God 12, 16, 18, 30, 36, 38, 45, 52, 72, 75, 100, 101, 112, 117
Holy Spirit 6, 38, 43, 59
holy wars 8, 93
hope vii, viii, xi, 21, 81, 82, 84, 87, 89, 90, 115, 117, 125
hostile 11, 28, 122
HS (Holy Spirit) 6, 16, 43
humanity 83

I

idolatry 32, 73
imperious 67
inferiority 16
inner peace 39
insane world ix, 43, 66, 75, 112-114, 119
insanity viii, x, 11, 43, 52, 53, 66, 67, 75, 82, 84, 85, 93, 101, 111, 112, 114, 115, 129
intelligence 30
intent viii, 60, 66, 73, 92, 93
interpersonal skills 93, 94, 97

J

Japan 43
Jewish viii, ix, x, 16, 51, 102
Jews killed Christ 51
job 6, 30, 43, 54, 71, 91, 92
Job (Biblical reference) 6
joy 1, 2, 3, 6, 7, 9, 10, 22-25, 28, 39, 53, 54, 57, 59, 61, 62, 64, 65, 67, 73, 75, 80, 89, 90
joyful divinity 47
joyous 52, 59

K

Kant, Immanuel 83
killing rabbits 34
Koran 8

L

law viii, 28, 42, 72, 81, 83, 84, 87, 89, 90
lawyer 34
lazy 8, 90, 122
learning 81, 83, 84, 87, 89, 90
life messages 82
little willingness 12, 43, 59, 62, 65, 66, 79, 80, 114
live in joy 73
look for the gift 15, 66

love 5-9, 12, 18, 19, 28, 56, 58, 60, 61, 64-67, 71, 72, 75, 81, 83, 84, 87, 89, 90, 111, 113, 114, 119, 122, 125, 129
    love minded 5, 9, 12
    loving belief system 62
    loving God 2, 18, 22, 24
low self esteem 8, 22, 24, 66, 125
Luther, Martin 82

M

Macklin, Charles 83
magic 34
man x, 11, 18, 47, 71-73, 77, 84, 89, 90, 100
manipulation 93
    manipulation skills 93
marriage viii, 114
materialistic 1, 12
    materialistic view 12
meaningful encounter 63
metaphysical 1
metaphysics 12
Middle East 8, 93
mind control 10, 11, 13, 16, 18
mind training 1, 10, 12, 35, 39, 80, 84, 85, 90
minds like rubber bands 86
ministers ix, 32, 115
minorities ix, 72
miracle 111-113
miraculous recoveries 21
mirror viii, 8, 11, 15, 60, 61, 102, 103, 120
    mirror reflection 120
    mirroring 15
money 12, 27, 29, 30, 39, 42-45, 47, 48, 51, 71-74, 84, 89-91, 122, 124, 125, 129
moral x, 85
    moral life 85
    morality 81, 83, 85, 87, 89, 90
mother viii, ix, 12, 59, 102, 119
motivation 2, 5, 7, 9, 10, 16, 21-24, 53, 78
    motivation systems 21
    motivational schools 21

N

negative viii, 3, 9, 15, 17, 20, 31, 45, 48, 52, 60, 65-67, 74, 80, 105, 109, 116-118, 129
    negative beliefs 109
    negative encounter 65

negative events 66
negative fears 117
negative feelings 105
negativity 66, 80, 117
Nietzsche 82
nightmare 6, 21, 43, 66
nightmare of this world 43
non-idolatry 32
non-judgmental 67
nutritionists 107

O

open 74-81, 87-89
openness 75-77, 79, 119
order of difficulty 120
organized religions 48
Ortega y Gasset, Jose 83, 85

P

pain vii, viii, ix, x, xi, 1-3, 6, 9, 15, 31, 38, 43, 57, 59, 60-62, 102, 115-119
past 46, 48, 65, 73, 90, 105
    past encounter 65
peace vii, xi, 5, 8, 12, 15, 22, 33, 34, 35, 36, 37, 38, 39, 46, 59, 61, 75, 89, 90, 102, 111,
    113, 114
people-skill training 97, 98
perception x, xi, 5, 7, 8, 11, 12, 21, 28-30, 39, 61, 93
perfection 32
perpetrator 48, 52
personality 28, 97, 98
    personality characteristics 95-97, 99
positive
    attitude 66
    gift 26, 27, 29
    mental attitude 21
power x, 2, 6, 8, 9, 21, 34, 36, 42, 43, 45, 48, 67, 68, 73, 89, 90, 114, 125
practice 59, 62, 66, 71, 99
priest ix, 8, 32, 48, 92, 102, 115
principal 21, 100
principle ix, x, 12, 22, 26, 47, 52, 54, 55, 59, 62, 67, 68, 71, 77, 84, 85, 90, 92, 94, 100,
    101, 126
professional 44, 74
project ix, 95, 122
projection ix, 62, 124
protector x, 102

punishment ix, 100, 101, 119

R

rabbit(s) 34-36, 39, 67
rationalized fear 77
real estate 67
reality x, xi, 5, 8, 11, 12, 28, 61, 83-85, 93, 102, 120, 125
reflection 22, 28, 65, 71, 80, 82, 96, 101, 120
rejecting 72, 122
relationship 34, 55-59, 61, 62, 64, 66, 71, 73, 75, 100, 102, 103, 114, 129
religion(s) 1, 6, 19, 48, 72, 114, 115
replacing life's struggle 67
resistance 10, 15
revenge 53, 55, 62, 82, 84
reward 70, 114
ridicule 78
root cause 35, 77, 93
ruthless 5, 8

S

saints and sinners 66
scores 10, 88
secrets 75, 77, 115
self defense 92
self esteem viii, x, 8, 22, 24, 28, 47, 48, 52-54, 59, 66, 67, 125, 129
self fufilling prophesy 129
separated 59, 67, 100, 119
separation 6, 11, 12, 36, 38, 43, 52, 54, 55, 59, 67, 73, 100, 101, 114, 117, 119, 129
    separation from God 6, 11, 36, 38, 43, 54, 67, 73, 100
seven questions 65
sex 18, 73
Shaw, George Bernard 82, 84
shoot to kill 93
single greatest fear 119
sinners 63, 64, 66, 93, 115
sins 62, 64, 66, 114
sister 12, 59, 90
sloppy 122
social 30, 43, 47, 58, 72, 126
    social acceptance 30
    social animal 72
    social bigotry 72
    social posturing 43
    social problems 72

soldier 92, 93, 101, 102, 109
special love 84
special relationship 34, 66
spiritual agendas 101
spiritual
    faith 5, 7, 9, 10
    gifts 18
    solutions 9
statistical accuracy 63
superiority 16
suspicious 80

T

therapists x, 32, 48
therapy viii, 8, 47, 48, 72
thinking 5, 9, 12, 35, 48, 70, 81, 83, 84, 87, 89, 90, 92, 124
this world viii, ix, x, 5-12, 18, 21, 22, 30, 38, 43, 44, 46, 52, 53, 65-68, 71-75, 77, 82, 84,
    85, 89, 90, 101, 111, 112, 114, 119, 129
thoughts of attack 92, 109
threshold question 114
tough minded 5, 9, 12
traditional religion 1, 114
truth xi, 1, 2, 82, 83, 85, 90, 100
turmoil 10, 72
turn the other cheek 12, 65, 66
twelve-step groups 48

U

UCLA Hospital 21
unachievable goal 125
uncle 59
universality 100
unrealistic expectancies 66

V

vendetta 101
vengeance 2, 82, 92
vengeful 18, 112, 115, 122
    vengefulness 18
victim 66, 67
viewpoint 73

W

war 6, 8, 101

wily 92
withdrawal 7, 80, 117
wolf in sheep's clothing 93
women ix, 72, 73, 124
work viii, x, 6, 9,-13, 15, 18, 19, 21, 26, 31, 36, 38, 65, 67, 73, 83-85, 88-93, 100, 107, 114, 117, 126, 129
workplace 91, 92
world of insanity 43
worldly
    ambitions 85
    emotion 119
worst fears 6, 52, 117

Order Blank

Name

Mailing Address

City

State   ZIP Code   Phone

Quantity

☐   Enclose a check or money order for $12.95 plus appropriate shipping charges (see below) for each book ordered. California residents add 7.75% sales tax.

SHIPPING
Domestic, add $2.00 for first book, and $0.50 for each additional book in the same order. International, add $5.00 for first book, and $1.00 for each additional book in the same order.

TOTAL ENCLOSED: $_____ . _____

Mail this form with payment to: Associates Publishers, 16776 Bernardo Center Dr., Ste. 110B, Rancho Bernardo, CA 92128

Please take a moment to share your feelings about this book with the author. Did *A Course in Miracles in 5 Minutes* help you? If so, how? All comments, whether positive or negative, are appreciated. Use the back of this form if you need more space.

_____

_____

_____

_____

_____

_____

(for volume discounts, contact Associates Publishers at 16776 Bernardo Center Dr., Ste. 110B, Rancho Bernardo, CA 92128)